Awakening Your Crystals

Activate the Higher Potential of Healing Stones

SHARON L. McALLISTER

EARTHDANCER

AN INNER TRADITIONS IMPRINT

For J, O, Stuart, Cameron, Angus and Ruaraigh

First edition 2019

Sharon L. McAllister
Awakening Your Crystals:
Activate the Higher Potential of Healing stones

This English edition © 2019 Earthdancer GmbH
Editing by JMS books LLP (www.jmseditorial.com)

Cover design: DesignIsIdentity.com
Cover photography: Karola Sieber
Typesetting and layout: DesignIsIdentity.com
Typeset in Whitman and Myriad

Printed and bound in China by Midas Printing Ltd.

ISBN 978-1-62055-972-7 (print)
ISBN 978-1-62055-973- 4 (e-book)

Published by Earthdancer, an imprint of Inner Traditions
www.earthdancerbooks.com, www.innertraditions.com

Contents

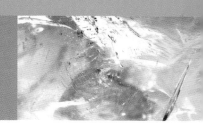

Disclaimer

I sincerely hope you enjoy all the practical crystal wisdom that is contained in this book. If you have any health concerns, I recommend that you consult with your doctor prior to beginning the crystal applications outlined. Medical intervention has saved my life on more than one occasion, therefore I have nothing but the greatest gratitude and respect for the medical treatment afforded to us all by doctors. My vision of hope, however, is that we find a way, on our planet, to embrace more wholeheartedly all aspects of the human energy field, particularly in our health challenges, healthcare, and any subsequent treatments required, and that care of the human energy field can partner advancing medical practice.

Crystals are noninvasive and therefore may be used positively alongside your medical treatment; however, for your own reassurance, always check with your doctor first. Crystals positively "change, charge, and enhance" the human energy field. "Dis-ease" begins in the energy field; unchecked, it can track into the physical body and establish there. It can take time for dis-ease to evolve in the physical body, and often our only choice is to seek the "quick fix" of drug medication. This may or may not be a help; however, with crystals there will always be some kind of change, charge, and enhancement of energy flow taking place. And if dis-ease has become entrenched in the physical body beyond the "tipping point," too far for a person to make a return to a healthy, fully flowing energy, please be assured that the crystals will have caused some positive energetic shift, even if the person using the crystals is not destined to get physically better, or perhaps may even be near the end of their life journey. That person will still have received an energy cleansing, together with a charge of energetic positivity that will enhance them and their energy field as they progress on their individual soul journey, whether that is in the direction of greater physical health or of soul completion.

Please do not combine crystal use with recreational drugs and/or alcohol. Positive use of crystals seeks to balance the four lower bodies and loading the body/energy field with toxins is counterproductive. I hope this clarifies the safe and positive use of crystals.

Sharon L. McAllister

Awakening your crystals

Awakening Your Crystals is a practical introduction to programming crystals in order to use their healing properties in an everyday way to keep you, your family, your home, and your environment positive and energetically free-flowing, promoting and enhancing your own health and well-being together with that of everyone around you.

Whether you are a beginner with regard to crystals, or a seasoned practicing holistic therapist, *Awakening Your Crystals* offers crystal programming suggestions that are alternative holistic healing solutions for a variety of everyday family health and well-being challenges.

If you have ever wished there was an alternative way to tackle a headache or backache, for example, or to help you and your child have a more peaceful night's sleep, or if you have ever wondered how to energetically protect your home, or wished you could begin to raise the positivity of your neighborhood—in other words, to remedy all the challenging "stuff" that life throws at us—then please consider the use of crystals to help you; there are many transformative crystal programming solutions offered within these pages.

This book is also for anyone who has held or seen crystals and pondered their role and existence. Where have they come from? How old are they? What do they do? Why do they do that? How can they do that? Why are we so fascinated by them? Why do children love them so much? Can they really help me and if so, how?

Awakening Your Crystals is a book for everyone. Even if you have never seen or handled crystals before, I believe that, after reading this book, you will feel confident to use them with the degree of respect and care appropriate to what you require of them. If you are a seasoned therapist, perhaps already well versed in your use of crystals, I believe there is additional useful information within these pages that can enhance your further development.

I hope that through this book, *Awakening Your Crystals*, we can all appreciate with greater understanding that a crystal is not just a pretty little rock, but rather a being, full of life, Light, and positive energy. I hope you find much to help your health and well-being within these pages.

I wish you well on your journey.
Sharon L. McAllister

Common questions asked about crystals

As we begin to look at how crystals evolved from the Earth and into our consciousness, I would like to make a suggestion. I appreciate that some crystal-aware readers may prefer to skip this chapter and head directly to the "Crystal Programming" section for help with alleviating a current problem such as a headache or backache. This is how I would like you to use this book, and I can well understand why you would wish to go straight to the information you need right now. If that is your aim at this moment, what I would say is that, as soon as you have some time, please come back and take a look at this chapter, because you may be surprised at some of the information about crystals that is contained here.

For those of you who are crystal therapists, developing your practice and further experience, you may feel that you are about to go over familiar ground. However, again, I would urge you not to skip this chapter, as I am sure there will be insights that will add to your bank of knowledge and be useful to you in your crystal work.

Whatever your future connection to crystals, hopefully you will enjoy having them around you and become confident to use them in your life to begin healing yourself, your family, your home, and your environment, as well as using them to enhance your personal journey of soul discovery.

What is a crystal?

A crystal is a physical manifestation of Light energy. A pure quartz crystal is a myriad of vibrations of Light and has many healing qualities. A rose quartz, for example, carries a specific vibration of Light, made physical, to embody and emit the Light of peace, healing, and unconditional love. Crystals are "Light beings," just like us.

What is crystal healing?

Crystal healing is the application of crystals to the body, and/or to the chakras, and/or the placement of crystals at key points in the energy field of the person being treated. The crystals are manifestations of Light and when they are "asked/programmed" they are "ignited" or charged with a magnification of Light energy that has the capacity to absorb negative energy in and around the body while charging the energy within and around the body with enhancing Light energy. This Light energy seeks to balance, harmonize, and positivize the energy bodies of the person receiving crystal healing.

Likewise, crystals perform the same transmutative and positive energy charge when directed at other tasks—for example, aligning mind, body, and spirit in your children, or raising the positive energy vibration and flow in your home or workplace, or healing sores on the Earth. The list of applications where crystal healing can better our lives is endless.

Do crystals have energy? If so, what is that?

Energy is everything. You are energy planted into a physical body and you use and apply your energy in a certain way. It is the same for a crystal; it is energy planted into a physical body and, like you, the universe has given each crystal a unique job to do. You give off energy. If you were to be photographed by Kirlian photography, for example, we would be able to see a basic and somewhat crude interpretation of your energy in that moment; the same applies to heat-sensitive photography. I am sure that, in time, energy photography will develop and improve and "seeing" crystal energy emission will be easier and clearer; yet be assured that, see it or not, the energy is there. The crystal pulses and radiates Light all around it and simultaneously has the capacity to "absorb" negative energy to the point of containment (see the chapter on Cleansing crystals, page 21).

As a crystal gives off positive energy and "breathes in" negative energy, it is rhythmic, pulsing, not unlike you and I as we breathe in and out; so the crystals breathe in and out, breathing in negative energy, breathing out Light.

Each crystal has a unique recipe of energy properties inherent in its being. A rose quartz, for example, has many therapeutic and healing energies about its natural energy makeup (an encyclopedia on rose quartz alone would fail to do justice to all that it can do) and key to its energetic properties is the vibration of "peace" and "healing." You cannot be near a rose quartz and not be affected by the energy it emits in waves of peace and healing. The same applies, of course, to other crystals and their own unique waves of energy emission radiating out around them.

So, how do crystals work and why?

Crystals work because they are a gift from the divine, from the universe, from the Earth energy, from Light, as are all natural gifts, given to us to enhance and promote our positivity. The divine universe has blessed our planet Earth with all we require to be fed and to drink, to have shelter, and to have peace and love for each other, yet over time we have successfully abused these gifts, both collectively and individually. Crystals are a cosmic gift to us to boost our healing potential, to promote our connection to Spirit, and to assist us to act responsibly for the negativity we create (see crystal car kits, page 99) so that we may take responsibility and transmute our negative energy.

The way in which crystals perform this remarkable task on our behalf is always to show us and remind us of "positive energy," so that we have a model of positive energy to follow in the pure vibration of Light; our own energy then recognizes this and, knowing what its true positive state should be, follows the model energy state of the crystal. So, for example, when your heart is closed and has "forgotten" how to open, try wearing a rose quartz over your heart chakra. This crystal will vibrate at a rate to show your depleted heart chakra: "This is how you can be, this is the beauty you can show, this is the way, this is the love, true and pure, that you can give, follow my example." Like a tuning fork striking a musical note to follow, the "molecular resonance" of the crystal vibrates to show the imbalance within you the equal and opposite positive energy, for the negative, dis-eased part of your energy field to follow.

The crystal strikes a vibration of pure energy, like the tuning fork, and says follow this note, follow this vibration of energy. Your energy, perhaps wobbly at first, perhaps in need of a number of sessions, begins to emulate the energetic vibrational note shown by the crystal. The crystal shows you the perfect mirror of pure energy vibration for your body and your energy field to become.

How old is a crystal?

Probably millions of years old.

Do I have a connection to my crystal?

Yes. It is likely that you did not choose it, rather that it chose you. It magnetized to your energy and sought to correct it, to "heal" you. It sensed a gap in your energy makeup and simply sought to fill it. If you have a great energy connection to a crystal, then perhaps you have worked together in other times and now you are reconnected to fulfil a job of healing together once more.

Why do I need to cleanse my crystal—it doesn't look dirty?

Crystals require cleansing because they are powerful tools for both magnification of energy and absorption of energy. If I take a sponge and dip it into inky water, it will draw up water and fill up the sponge; once filled to saturation point, the sponge begins to drip back the water it can no longer contain and has thus gone beyond its point of saturation. This is exactly what happens with crystals. So, if you wear an amethyst for healing your emotional energy, you certainly would not wish to have that accumulation of negative emotional energy dripping back into your energy field. Rather, I am sure you would wish to release your negativity fully, transmuting the feelings. Therefore, we all have to be responsible and cleanse our crystals accordingly. (See the chapter on Cleansing crystals, page 21, as there are many varied methods to suit your particular crystal use.)

How can I get my crystal to work for me?

Simply "ask" your crystal, as asking is a form of programming. If you ask your crystal while holding it in your right palm (in terms of energy with regard to hands, it is "right to receive," "left to leave," thus the left palm is often used for sweeping away energy in healing), your crystal will respond to that request only, as long as it is positive and within the energy remit of the crystal. Think of this analogy: I ask you to plumb in my sink. If you are a plumber, that is fine; if you are not, well, you may have a go, but how effective would you be? The crystal always works best and most efficiently in the area of its universal remit; thus, it will always work with a high degree of energy amplification if asked/programmed to do so. If a crystal is never programmed, it is working but at its lowest volume. If you ask/program the crystal, it is charged, ready to ignite its empowerment to apply its energy to the task; you have magnified its Light charge many times over.

What actually happens when I hold my crystal and "ask"?

Let's say you have a rose quartz pendant and want to ask/program this pendant to veil you with peace when you wear it. You hold the pendant in your right hand and say: *I ask the Light [or Earth energy, if you prefer] that this rose quartz veil me with the Light of peace. Thank you.*

You may say to yourself when reading this: Hang on a minute, I'm holding a rock in my hand and I'm asking it to veil me with the energy of peace? How does that work? It sounds fantastical, doesn't it! And it is. The reason it sounds so fantastical is that we have forgotten that everything is energy. We have forgotten we are energy. Many of us believe we are only physical bodies trotting about on the planet and that is it—nothing more, yet we are so much more. In reality, we are energy inhabiting a physical body and a crystal is energy inhabiting a rock or stone.

At the point at which you program a crystal, your energy meets the crystal energy (now resting in the palm of your hand) and something important happens. Your energy puts its "feelers" out (see box).

In truth, your energy always has its "feelers" out. Think about anywhere you may have been that didn't "feel" right. Maybe, to you, it didn't feel good. Maybe it even felt like a place you did not want be in. That is your intuition at work, your energy with its feelers out, always sensing, always assessing the energy around you, even if you are not actually paying attention to this energetic messaging.

Have you ever stood next to someone, maybe you didn't even look at that person, but you experienced a shudder going through you, or a feeling of wanting to shrink back, or a sensation that you wanted to move away? You don't know this person or anything about them, but you have a "feeling." That is because your energy field—your "four lower bodies," which are all around your body, ending at arm's length—is responding to the energy it meets, all the time, and if you stop to think how many people pass within arm's length of your body in a day, perhaps on the train to work, queuing for coffee, or in the supermarket, then that is a lot of people moving in and around your own personal energy field. Some of those people will be lovely, kind-hearted individuals and some will not. So it is hardly surprising that you may shudder, or feel that you want to retract your energy, well away from someone who is negative. Whether we like the idea or not, we are energy and we need to learn to take care of our energy and keep our own individual energy fields in the most positive, Light-aligned, healthy flow that we are able to muster.

Let's return to you, holding the crystal that you have just asked/programmed to veil you with the energy of peace. "Asking" is a vibrational call. Energy follows thought. Energy follows words. Energy follows deeds. So, in your asking, a pattern of vibrational energy meets the energy of the crystal and "patterns" it to what is required. It is like coding for your computer. You ASK and you are coding for a crystal. The crystal patterns to its vibrational requirement, as you have asked it to do, therefore releasing its "tuning fork" capacity. It strikes the required vibrational note, depending upon its remit (for example, rose quartz = the vibration of peace), and immediately the crystal's energy meets your energy; it begins to hum its vibration of energy through you and around you and your energy is drinking in that crystal energy, sensing that charge of positivity, sensing the absorption of negativity away from your energy field, together with the harmonizing balance of feeling cleaner and clearer—even if you have no cognitive awareness of this happening.

When you ask/program the crystal, you are calling on the Light (or the Earth energy, if you prefer) to charge the crystal with the "empowerment of Light," thus asking that the crystal be ignited for a particular positive purpose; so, for example, to bring you the energy of peace, the Light (the highest positive vibrational energy in the universe) ignites your rose quartz.

The Light wants to positivize your energy, wants to positivize the planet's energy.

All we have to do is Ask.

Why would the Light help me?

Why does the Light, the highest positive vibrational energy in the universe, want to positivize our energy? Because we come from Light. We are Light. We are Light energy inhabiting physical bodies on this planet of free will, Earth, completing incarnations or rounds of experience, after which we return to our real home—the Light.

Crystals are Light energy, like us, in a physical body (rock/stone), and their Light energy has a resonance to our energy, therefore "crystalline energy" can enhance our own energy in a myriad of ways, depending on the crystal's energy remit and on what your own energy requires to balance and positivize it to its most harmonious state at any given time.

Do crystals have any importance in our modern times?

Crystals have always been important to the Earth and to those who inhabit the Earth in every age, yet through many ages of our planet they have lain dormant, hidden away from us beneath the earth, recognized by those who intuited their vibrational capacity and ability to enhance their lives and kicked aside by those who only saw rocks.

There have been great "crystalline ages" on our planet. In our tech-savvy times, names like Lemuria or Atlantis seem more like made-up stories or strange myths that could not possibly have any kind of reality attached to them, and yet those great crystalline ages did in fact occur. There really was a Lemuria and Atlantis. So why does any of that matter now? It matters because, like the fall of any great past civilization, we can learn something important from its demise.

Both Lemuria and Atlantis harnessed new technologies for their respective ages. The technologies that developed centrally to their civilizations were crystal-powered; however, they misused their gift of technology, used this empowerment negatively, and both civilizations fell in self-destruction.

We stand at a tipping point on our planet Earth right now. We have developed technologies that have damaged our Earth, that continue to wreak devastation every day, that harm us in mind, body, and spirit, and yet we continue to move into our absorption of self-focus for all the wrong reasons. For example, many seek ego, vanity, or instant fame through social media rather than a self-focus to progress our own healing, to grow and nurture our wisdom, and to further our positive development. We have ignored the universal gift of crystal energy, quite literally laid at our feet in our age, except to use crystals in the form of silicon for chips that conduct energy and power all the phones, tablets, laptops, and gadgets that we deem so essential in our lives.

How many times might you hear someone say: "I can't live without my cell phone" or "Social media is my life. I can't live without it."

We like such toys, whether we use them for good or instead allow them to control or damage us, or even allow ourselves to become addicted to them. We have in fact done all of this before—in Lemuria and Atlantis.

And so here we stand today and the benevolent universe, ever generous, ever manifold, has gifted us the so-called New Age, often derided by scientists and Silicon Valley techy folk because they are gleefully embracing only one side of the New Age, riding the technology wave no matter where it takes them—and us along with them. It may take us to "kingdom come," but let's hope not.

We should instead be embracing the New Age by learning to balance and positivize ourselves, our families, our homes, and our environments; by learning to balance our beautiful planet Earth, by keeping that key question to the fore of our focus at all times, in all we think, say, and do: "Does this action bring balance, harmony, positivity, and betterment to me and those around me, near and far?"

Crystals exist to balance and positivize ourselves and our planet. They are an important key to your health and well-being. They are noninvasive and they work well alongside most conventional medical treatments to support your journey to health. They raise the positive energy in your home, your garden, your street, your town. Crystals can heal wounds and sores on the Earth; for example, where battles and terrible events have occurred. Crystals can support us and enhance our lives in so many ways, if only we would choose to use them.

I am not sure how crystals can possibly benefit or affect me?

If you are unsure or even a disbeliever in the healing power of crystals, let me remind you that crystals are all around you already. Crystals consume much of your every waking moment, potentially bringing huge benefits to your life in a physically gratifying way; indeed, they already affect your everyday life more than you give them credit for. That is because it is a humble crystal, called silicon, that goes to make up the "silicon wafer" (more commonly referred to as the IC, chip, or microchip) that is the main component in all things digital. You would not have equipment such as your cell phone and your laptop without this silicon crystal. Therefore, what I am asking you is: If we can all embrace the capability of this crystal, silicon, why can we not embrace the "superconductive" capabilities of other crystals, which can be super-helpful and super-revolutionary to us in our lives through their capacity to "conduct" vibrational energy and healing energy, absorbing, transmuting, promoting positive energy that can help us in infinite ways, and, to begin with, in some of the everyday ways outlined in these pages?

I hope this book goes some way toward illustrating the benefits of crystal energy, particularly to those who would not usually find crystals of interest. I hope that these people, in particular, will find it in their hearts to be open-minded about the subject, for this is a collection of "crystal wisdom" that can bring about practical, positive change in your life.

Let's get started

Before we look at the basic information required to begin crystal healing, I would like to outline the differences between the "personal" crystal practitioner and the "professional" crystal practitioner.

In my understanding, the most important difference between the two is when it comes to programming a crystal. Information for the more advanced or professional user appears against a purple background throughout the book.

If I am working with crystals at home for personal interest, on my children or maybe my dog, for example, I can keep things very simple. The crystal practitioner's responsibilities toward their client are different. I am at home, using simple crystal programming and working with care and responsibility on my children and my dog—my children and animals love crystals, so everyone is happy.

However, if I am working as a professional crystal therapist, I have a greater "karmic responsibility" to myself and to those who come before me for crystal healing. Therefore, I am required by the Light to work at a more responsible level, with "Light understanding," because I am a "Lightworker." I will have a greater responsibility to care for the person coming before me for crystal healing and I will probably be working with more complex and powerful configurations of "crystal circuitry" (see page 43).

There is a quick reference chart for programming at the end of each chapter on the eight key crystals recommended for the toolkit, then more ideas for programming later in the book in the section on important crystals and their energy attributes (page 132). In the section on programming crystals (page 42), I have included two sets of programs: templates for crystal programs for all the items where there is a more personal, home, or family-related focus of crystal healing, together with templates for crystal programs for those undertaking professional crystal healing. Please use the program/s you feel most drawn to.

Cleansing crystals

There are many myths about crystal healing, in particular about crystal cleansing and crystal care. I have received long, detailed descriptions from people about how they cleanse and care for their crystals, some of which may seem pointless or off-putting to anyone considering work-ing with crystals. Simple techniques and an approach based on accu-racy, brevity, and clarity work best, but remember it is important to regularly cleanse the crystals that you wear and/or use for energy work.

The methods of crystal cleansing I will outline have a difference—only because if you use and work with crystals professionally, then you will have to work harder. I will begin with personal use and work up, and as you read through the techniques the differences between personal use and professional use should become clear.

Cleansing crystals for personal use

Let's say I have a couple of pendants I like to wear: a rose quartz and a turquoise. The rose quartz is mounted in gold and the turquoise in silver, and I wear them on gold and silver chains respectively.

Gold-mounted pendants may be quickly, lightly washed in water and patted dry with a clean natural fiber cloth—cotton or linen. They should then be put in a "light" place, on a pure cotton cloth on a table in sunlight, for example, and given a rest from being worn for at least three hours. If you have the intention (remember, energy follows thought) then *your intention* to energy-cleanse your crystal of *your* absorbed negativity will be sufficient that the crystal, when rinsed in pure clear water, will release the held negativity.

You should do this daily, or as often as you wear the pendant.

For the turquoise pendant, set in silver, it is best not to wet or soak the stone in water, as both the stone and the silver setting may tarnish easily. For this stone, you can choose from other cleansing methods.

The amethyst bed

An amethyst bed is a natural piece of amethyst quartz crystal, in a reasonably flat open shape upon which you may safely rest other crystals.

An amethyst bed should be placed on the windowsill, or in sunlight, with the turquoise (or other) pendant upon it for at least three hours (twelve hours maximum). During this time, the sunlight works with the amethyst to cleanse and draw from the stone (in this case, turquoise) the held negativity and to absorb and transmute it. Likewise, moonlight cleansing transmutes challenging emotional holding. After the turquoise is removed from the amethyst bed, it is important that you place the amethyst bed into water for cleansing. Place in a glass bowl in natural light for twelve hours to cleanse the amethyst of held negativity, then replace it on the windowsill for recharging. Do not worry if you have no actual sunlight—daylight will suffice.

Pyramid cleansing

A gold wire pyramid or a glass pyramid will suffice for this method. Do not use another type. Place your pendant on the base, in the center, and do not cleanse more than three pendants at a time. The pendants should rest within the apex vortex of the pyramid for three to twelve hours in natural light and then may be worn as desired. *Always cleanse the pendant after you have worn it.*

Salt crystals (sea salt)

Many people I know cleanse crystals in sea salt water. It is good with some crystals but is not necessary for pendants. Instead, cover the surface of a glass platter or plate (at least 6-inch/15cm diameter) with large, coarse sea salt granules. Then put a clean, white or natural, 100 percent pure fiber cotton or linen cloth on the sea salt bed and place your pendant(s) upon it, with a maximum of three pendants. Place in natural light for a minimum of three hours and dispense with the sea salt after use. Wash the cloths and wear the pendants as you choose.

If you are not using, displaying, or wearing your crystals, then place them in a drawer. A midnight blue velvet pouch or wrap would be appropriate to contain and protect them. At this point, your crystals will revert to a dormant status. (See the section on the three states of being, page 28.)

Cleansing of lamps and crystal artefacts for the garden

Lamps may be placed on a bed of sea salt as previously described; and artefacts that are outside, say in a garden, will be naturally energy-cleansed by the elements.

Cleansing crystals for professional therapist use

Cleansing crystals if you are a practicing crystal therapist is another matter entirely. Here you have taken on the karmic responsibility to use crystals to charge the energy field of another.

We could consider that *you* will never heal anyone and *I* will never heal anyone. However, if we do our jobs carefully, we might help someone else to heal themselves. I will only ever heal me. You will only ever heal you. Yet you and I may be blessed to encounter along the way people who help us in our personal healing and who through "holistic therapy" will help us release our negativity; counsel us to be empowered in our positivity; align us to accept personal responsibility; and help us to connect to our angels, guides, and masters in the Light, that we may take up a soul connectedness in our lives, recognize the soul, the "divine plan," and learn to flow with the beauty of life and to make choices in connection with our divine selves, no matter how hard we perceive them to be. To entrust ourselves to divine Light. To be Light.

The healing of another should never be undertaken without great respect. There are many intuitive and gifted people who have a great capacity to heal, yet who damage their energy field at each "healing" encounter because they have never learned to cleanse and protect their own energy field. If you have a gift—and in truth everyone has a gift to heal, everyone can be a "conduit of Light"—it is not you, it is the Light energy you will conduct. If you are a smoking, swearing, beer-swilling-every-night type of person, yet potentially a great healer, your energy field will be clouded and not flowing, and you will be showing your lack of humility, respect, and understanding of the Light energy that potentially may flow through you to help others. We must all take care not to incur karma for any lack of due respect.

Professional crystal healing is an advanced level therapy and much working knowledge of the human energy field is required, together with a high degree of personal attainment. The therapist has to have a "strong and clean" energy to withstand working with crystals on other people.

I recommend that crystal therapists train intensively on top of another therapy discipline—they may already be a reiki healer or reflexologist, for example. Competent training and understanding of the anatomy of the energy field are very important. If you are choosing a local course for yourself, go and talk to the tutors; "feel" their wisdom. You will intuit whether it is the right course for you, or if the environment is right for you to begin your learning journey.

Good spiritual housekeeping

Professional therapist cleansing routine
- Meditate twice daily.
- Align and protect your energy regularly throughout the day.

Alignment of the self
- Stop and be still.
- Call to the Light for help ("I call upon the Light, please help me at this time…").
- Breathe away the negativity from your body and your energy field, from the crown of your head to your feet and away into the earth for transmutation (for example, visualize the color blue, washing from the crown to the feet and out into the earth).

- Breathe in the Light of positivity and connection to Spirit (for example, the color emerald washing from the crown to the feet, grounding your Light to the earth and through the arms to the hands).
- Seal yourself in protective blue light (for example, draw a veil of blue light over the crown, at arm's length from the body, and see it veil all around you in an "egg" shape, sealing beneath the feet.
- Be of joy and positivity.

Cleanse and align your home and your workspace several times a day. Use the method described earlier: call on the Light to breathe the negativity away from the room, all objects within the room, and yourself, and release it to the earth for transmutation. For example: *I call upon the Light, please cleanse this room, all objects of this room, and myself of all negative energy. Please release this negative energy to the earth for transmutation. I thank the Light.*

Then call on the Light: *I call upon the Light, please veil this room/ house, all objects of this room/house, and myself with the highest positivity for the energy required. I thank the Light.*

Always cleanse yourself and your space using the above alignment techniques *before* and *after* every healing session.

Cleanse your crystals *before* and *after* each healing session: in water; via an energy cleansing method; hands-on (only do this if you are very aligned and a competent practitioner).

The hands-on cleansing method

- Align yourself and cleanse your space.
- Place the crystals on a natural fiber cloth, on a table, before you.
- Align yourself again and call upon the Light to cleanse the crystals of all negative energy and release the negative energy to the earth for transmutation.
- As you are doing this, rub your palm chakras together, igniting your own energy, and sweep your palms three times over the crystals and then directionally sweep the negative "cloud" down

to the earth, literally dropping the energy from your hands, by your sides, onto the earth. Then sweep your own palms three times to the earth, releasing any residue of negativity from your palms. Ask that the earth receive the negative energy for transmutation and thank the earth.

- Then call upon the Light to recharge the crystals to the highest "positivity."

Storing crystals

There is an optimum way to store your crystals. Think of crystals in color families and keep those families together. Color in energy terms is vibrational healing in its own right. All pink crystals, for example, are working on the pink/rose ray of healing, so despite these crystals having their own individual healing remits, they can happily be stored together until they are required for use.

Storage of powerful crystal tools

Always store clear quartz crystal (ignitor) and smoky quartz crystal (exit) separately and never with points aimed at each other. It is better to store these powerful crystals side by side (this is because in crystal circuitry there is a magnetic pull when the points are aligned toward each other, therefore the crystals are restive, even when not in use, unless placed side by side).

A note on crystal storage for therapists

Personal crystals should always be kept separate from a working toolkit used to heal others. If you need to travel with your kit, wood can be expensive and heavy to carry. Workboxes from DIY stores are good, such as an electrician's box, and some even have wheels and handles, which are so great if you need to take all your kit with you. For family trips I always travel with a type of jewelry roll that includes an essential set of crystals to try to meet every eventuality on any given excursion.

Crystals and the three states of being

A crystal has three "states" of being: "dormant," "active," and "ignited." Here is a simple overview of the three states of being of a crystal.

Think of the "dormant" state of a crystal as being asleep. When you are asleep, you are resting, reserving energy, breathing lightly, recharging your energy. It is almost the same for a crystal—it is in a positive yet resting state where energy is being conserved for greater future use.

Think of the "active" state of a crystal as being awake. You are alert and ready; a greater flow of energy and activity is emanating from you now. This is the same for the crystal, except there is nothing general about its energy emanation; it has a specific role and job to do and will activate its energy direction or magnetize its energy emanation only when the opposite or resonant energy meets its field.

Think of the "ignited" state as the Light charging a crystal for a particular healing purpose. This crystal has been called into direct service with a programmed focus. Programming a crystal means it is invested with a "focus of energy" in order that it may direct that energy in healing action. What is healing? By healing we mean to cleanse, transmute, and eradicate negative energy and bring about energetic positivity, energetic harmony, and energetic flow in its place. The "ignited" crystal is fully powered, fully switched on to perform the task it has been charged with, and in this state, it is able to do a hundred times what it can do in its "active" state. That means a hundred times more powerful in both "energy absorption" (pulling in negativity from the energy field) and "magnification" (radiating out positive energy). Because of this fully powered state, this crystal will be working hard and require regular cleansing, followed by reprogramming and reigniting if required.

To expand on the three states of crystal being, I should explain that the crystal that lies beneath the earth evolves and is mined/

harvested when its life plan decrees it is time to be "birthed"—much the same as us, in fact. At the time of its birth to the earth surface, it has a live but dormant status. This means it has all the faculties of energy properties that it requires for its life and work on earth; it has a life plan and a planned connection to people/places/precise times (again, just like you). Yet the power of its energy and potential is not yet ignited; this dormant status remains until it connects to key people/places/timing in its destined life plan.

A rose quartz journey

Let's imagine a rose quartz: this crystal has taken 2.8 million years to evolve (yet, remember, some can grow in mere weeks) to the point of discovery and birth from the earth. At the point of birth, the rose quartz has living energy but is dormant, and yet it will still radiate great positivity as it is newly freed from the purity of its connection to the earth mother, who has created it. There is sadness too, because those involved in this part of the crystal's life are frequently "non-knowing" in matters of energy and do not understand what they do. They have no respect for the beauty and sensitivity of the wonders of the earth, nor respect for the earth mother's manifold gifts of healing and nurturance.

This particular rose quartz travels far, not usually in energy-sensitive circumstances; it is loaded, bundled, thrown, hacked at, hewn by sand and water, polished, sometimes carved, either well or grotesquely and inappropriately to the majesty of its being. The rose quartz reaches a local warehouse in Brazil, for example, and is purchased by, let's say, a dealer from England. The rose quartz then continues its journey, traveling unceremoniously again across seas and roads, even by air, until it reaches the UK wholesaler, who then sells it on to the retailer. Imagine how many negative energies have attached themselves to this "new baby" rose quartz, freshly hewn from the earth; it is not hard to imagine that on a scale of 1–10, many people handling this new crystal would be of low positivity, perhaps even quite negative. A blessing then that our rose quartz has been dormant and has had the protection of the "seal of energy" of its dormant state.

The rose quartz: dormant

The dormant state is new, in the sense that pre-Atlantis we did not have dormant crystals; our new baby rose quartz crystal would have been born out of the earth in an active state, because in pre-Atlantis times humans were much more developing Light beings, in finer, purer bodies. Back then, we could withstand being around active crystals; in fact, we adored, loved, and craved to be around active crystals. It was like being plugged in and on a "high" during the whole time we were with our crystals. Part of the fall of Atlantis was due to our manipulation of this high energy. In our time on this planet, our scientists play with cloning and genetically modify and generally poison our food chain and in Atlantis we went through a similar evolvement and science, with increasing greed, total self-focus, and lack of spirituality, ethics, or personal responsibility to others and the planet. As a consequence, this amazing and, in many ways, success-ful civilization fell. The crystals imploded, exploded, dematerialized, left the planet, sank into the planet, and cataclysmic events ensued on many levels, geographically, geologically, and karmically.

For all of us now living on this planet it means that this veil of "dormancy" protects us from doing great damage. Many people who use crystals do not truly understand the power of crystals and their correct use, nor is there a wide understanding of how to cleanse crys-tals effectively.

Examine the illustrations opposite and see the dormant energy state, the active energy state, and the ignited energy state. Note the layering of the attached energy for a crystal that is not yet cleansed.

Please remember it is important to cleanse your crystals.

Rose quartz
"dormant" state

Rose quartz
"active" state

Rose quartz
"ignited" state

That is not to say that the people and places on the journey of our rose quartz have not received any benefit; on the contrary, they will have benefited enormously. Each time they handle the stones they will be letting layers of their negativity release, shedding repeatedly, like an onion skin, fine layers of negative energy, which in turn are being absorbed by the crystal. If they have a weak and susceptible energy field, they may pick up on the imprints of others who have handled the stones. This is true for you too. Always *call* upon the Angels of Protection before handling crystals or stones. I rarely touch crystals or stones that belong to others. If I have to, I will ask for extra help from the Angels of Protection as I feel, quite literally, as if I have been burned (for my own learning experience) by the crystals of others, where the crystals have held a powerful negative energy imprint and have not yet been cleansed properly and effectively.

Remember—it is important also to seal and protect your own energy field from the negative energy imprints of others. (See Alignment of the self, page 39.)

The rose quartz: active

Once your rose quartz has reached your local crystal shop, it awaits you patiently. People can feel a very strong attachment and connection to their crystals and for whom certain ones in particular are very precious and special. Even though they feel this resonance and connectedness to the crystal, they often cannot grasp the idea that over millions of years the pathway of this crystal has evolved in order for it to connect with them at this particular moment. It is hard to imagine but a mutual evolvement has led to a given point in time in which we and our crystals connect. You are special and important, and to meet your importance another special 'Light' being, wearing the body of a crystal, has come millions of years and sometimes millions of miles to meet you. This crystal is a friend and, as such, we should treat it with respect.

Perhaps you go into your local crystal shop one day, rummage around in the box of rose quartz, and "choose" your friend (the rose quartz has actually helped you here, in this situation, by magnetizing to your energy). I have seen crystals in boxes quite literally "jump" toward a person to ensure they are collected by the right one. Then the magic happens: the instant *you* touch *your* crystal in the box, the crystal you choose, the one that is right for you, becomes active.

That is why if you have been stuck (the mind enters here rather than the intuition) choosing between two different crystals (you like this particular one but, hey, that one's pretty too), the very fact that you have touched the crystal causes it to change its state of being. It becomes active, thus its magnification of "energy resonance" to you is higher. I have seen people put down "their" crystal and choose the "pretty" one, only to return later (I have actually witnessed people in tears at this point) to collect "their" crystal because the pull of energy is so great, they simply must be together. If you have not yet started to use crystals, you can be forgiven for thinking that this is very strange; however, such is the power of energy.

A pyrite journey

In the active state, the crystal and you have ribbons of "Light attachment," spirals of energy that connect between you. These are positive, if treated with respect and positive intent, and will help to feed and nurture your energy field and physical body with a high charge of positive energy flow.

For example: take a pyrite "crystal." (There is nothing "crystalline" about the appearance of pyrite, sometimes known as "fool's gold"—it is a metallic-looking stone that comes in small cubes and large rocks but behaves as a crystal, so we will call it such for the purposes of this book.) It is a wonderful positive energetic resource to have about the home and has a long list of energy capabilities. Some of its key qualities are:

- To absorb, transmute, and positivize negative electromagnetic emissions, for example, television, microwave, cell phone, and computer electromagnetic emissions.
- To absorb, transmute, and positivize blocks in the human energy field connected to stubborn holding of negativity, particularly mental and emotional.

The pyrite: active

Imagine that a pyrite is stolen one day from the crystal shop. It is dropped and picked up by another person; they like the look of it, take it home, and place it on the windowsill in the kitchen. The pyrite is now active (although this was not its first choice of human being to connect to), and here, in its new situation, its energy meets a great and high negative charge within the room. There is a kettle, toaster, electric oven, microwave, washer, dryer, telephone, and sometimes a cell phone. The pyrite rises to the challenge, for it is a job it can do and do well, for a limited time; it can absorb all the "electromagnetic energy" in this place. If you could see this energy emitting from your appliances, it would look like sparking lightning moving not vertically, but horizontally, crackling and hitting the walls. The pyrite is not cleansed—if it were cleansed, it could be far more effective in its absorption of all this electromagnetic negativity flying about. Children walk within this energy (children have more vulnerable energy fields). The pyrite is limited in its power to absorb all this negativity emitted from appliances when its energy capacity is full, because, like the saturated sponge that drips the water it cannot hold back into the bucket, the pyrite, sadly, drips the negative energy it can no longer hold back into the atmosphere.

The pyrite: ignited

Yet if the pyrite is charged and programmed, it is not only active, it is ignited and in this state, it is able to do around a hundred times more than it can in its simple active state. However, to program the pyrite, to ignite its energy, requires some basic understanding of crystal energy and the care and respect required to deal with its greatly enhanced power. If the pyrite can absorb one hundred times that of its active state, it will be very powerful, pulling in and absorbing negativity from far around, and after doing this hard work the pyrite will require very regular cleansing followed by appropriate reprogramming/reigniting. Then the pyrite fulfils its destiny and realizes its reason for being, true to its purpose in the universe.

I hope this example illustrates to you the difference between the three states of being of a crystal: dormant, active, and ignited. It does not matter what kind of crystal or what purpose—personal wear, environmental, or other; when it comes to crystals, it is important to clean them, to respect them, to care for them, and to do no harm.

I should also clarify the point around the ignited crystal and its energy magnification. Energy magnification is a moveable measure and is dependent on many things, including the clarity and intent of the program, not to mention the connection to Light of the programmer; a crystal healer working with great knowledge, humility, respect, experience, and connection to "Light beings," who are sponsoring him/her in the crystal work they undertake, will have a greater energy conduit to charge a crystal, say, than the average man in the street. However, do not be put off if you are *not* a healer or crystal therapist; to learn to program and care for a crystal can be simple and joyous and the results incredible. Remember, if the energy magnification of that pyrite was even twice its active state, the crystal would still be very competently absorbing the negative energy of electromagnetic frequency emitted by our potentially damaging appliances.

Crystals and the human energy field

Everything has an energy. The trees. The sky. The chair you sit on. Your dog. Your goldfish. The road you drive to work on. The car you drive to work in. You have an energy field, whether you know you do or not. Whether you like the idea or not.

The human energy field is made up of many bands; however, for the purposes of the types of crystal healing we are focusing on in this book, we need to look at the four bands of energy that make up the four lower bodies of the human energy field: those that sit around the body, beginning nearest the body with the "physical energy" band, the "emotional energy" band layered over that, and then the "mental energy" band, finishing with the "spiritual energy" band, which usually completes at around arm's length away from the body.

Illustration of the human energy field

The illustration on page 35 shows the "blue etheric energy" immediately beyond the skin (literally showing the spirit in the body), which merges into the green of the "physical energy" band about ½ inch (1cm) around the body. The green of the physical energy band merges into the pink of the "emotional energy" band, which in turn merges into the yellow of the "mental energy" band, and this in turn merges into the blue of the "spiritual energy" band.

When looking at this diagram, it is important to remember that this is an illustration of a clean and clear, healthy, ideal energy field because, in truth, each of us has an energy field in constant flux, affected by our every thought, word, and deed; affected by our surroundings and the people around us, their energy and how it meets ours. Is the energy that meets ours positive? Or does it hook into ours, drain us, leave us depleted? Do we know people who "steal" our energy, who are happily plugging into our energy field because we have left it open and unguarded, and their depleted energy seeks to soak up ours as it is openly available? Equally, how great is anyone's individual energy field? For most of us, the energy field is not recognized or acknowledged and therefore it is not cared for at all. Yet would we leave the house without brushing our teeth? Or live in a house that we never cleaned?

This illustration features a heavy cannabis user. On his throat, the chakra is closed, showing a dark plume of negative energy around the lungs also. His stomach is showing the plume of dark red negative energy, indicating a dis-eased energy field. He has heavy, dark plumes of negative energy around his head, indicating mental fogging; the dark plumes around his knees denote

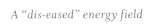

A "dis-eased" energy field

reluctance and stubbornness to move forward. The heavy clouds of negative energy on his shoulders denote physical burdens and his base chakra is blocked. He has depleted, narrow energy bands, while the outer "spiritual energy" band appears a dirty blue, indicating he is literally in a "dark cloud" and losing his spiritual connection. His "emotional energy" band is overpowered by his "mental energy," signifying that he is mentally directed in life, while any emotional capability of "feeling" is becoming less and less.

How big is each energy band?

In general, the band that sits closest to the body is the physical energy band or the physical sheath. This sits between 3 and 6 inches (7.5–15cm) above and around the whole body. If you are ill, this energy will be thin and discolored, perhaps with clouds of "dis-ease" within the banding. If you are healthy and physically fit, this band will be more robust and a cleaner, clearer color.

The emotional energy band rests another 6 inches (15cm) beyond the physical energy band and a healthy emotional energy band will be a clean, clear pink color. If a person is upset, darker flares and spikes will erupt within the emotional energy field. A person starved of love will have a thin, perhaps very depleted emotional energy band.

The mental energy band sits further out from the body, around 9 inches (23cm) beyond the emotional energy band, and should ideally be a clean, clear, golden yellow color. A person with headaches will have thick, stagnant, darker energy around the head sitting in this banding. If the headaches are like migraines, then that cloud of negativity will look murky and spiky, reaching out into other bands of energy surrounding the body.

The spiritual energy band sits a further 12 inches (30cm) out and should be a clean, clear blue color. This banding sits as a protective fourth sheath around the other three energy bodies. It is helpful to focus on this spiritual energy body, to see it as a blue ray of Light surrounding the body and see yourself veiled within its protective shield. I find it useful to imagine in my mind's eye that I am drawing a veil of blue Light around me, at arm's length, from up above the crown of the head, out around the body, and sealing beneath the feet, like a shield or a protective cloak. This is a positive focus to use at the beginning of the day, before you get out of bed, if you can.

We receive an "energetic increment of Light" for the day, each day at 6am. This is why many people who are spiritually connected meditate through the 6am point in the day. They are connecting to Light at the point they receive their energetic increment of Light. How many of us have "spent" our gift of Light energy before we even get to breakfast? If we imagine that carrying our Light is like carrying a cup of something precious around with us, how many of those precious drops of our Light would be lost before we even leave the house in the morning? How Light-filled are we in the melee of getting our boisterous children ready and out to school? How Light-filled are we driving through morning traffic madness? Drawing a cloak or shield of the blue ray of Light around the body at arm's length holds in your positive energy and helps you keep your Light energy tank fuller for longer.

Crystals are wonderful tools to use to enhance the health and well-being of the human energy field.

Preparing yourself for crystal energy work

Personal use

Before you program a crystal, it is important to ready yourself for the Light task.

Simply sit or stand quietly. Take a moment to focus on becoming peaceful and attuned to begin to work with crystals. Then ask that the Light (or the earth energies, if you prefer) cleanse you of all negativity. Then ask that the Light veils you with positivity and prepares you to begin crystal work. Then you are ready to program a crystal for your use, or your family's use, clear of any negative energy imprint you may have gathered through the day.

For example: *I ask the Light [or earth energies, if you prefer] to cleanse me of all negativity. I ask the Light to veil me with positivity and prepare me for crystal healing myself [or full name of other person here]. Thank you.*

It is important to use full names in Light work as your name carries an energetic vibration.

Professional use

Remember, preparation is important as you need to meet your client with your own energy as clean, clear, and aligned as possible.

Usually, professional crystal therapists will have meditated in preparation for each of their clients, connecting to the Light for insights into what is required for their clients' particular healing sessions on the day in question.

Alignment of the self

- Stop your activities and be still.
- Call to the Light for help.
- Breathe away the negativity from your body and your energy field from the crown of your head to your feet and away into the earth for transmutation (for example, visualize the color of blue, washing from the crown to the feet and out into the earth).
- Breathe in the Light of positivity and connection to Spirit (for example, the color emerald washing from the crown to the feet, grounding your Light to the earth and through the arms to the hands).
- Seal yourself in protective blue light (for example, draw a veil of blue light over the crown, at arm's length from the body, and see it veil all around you in an egg shape, sealing beneath the feet).
- Be of joy and positivity.

Alignment of the room

- Align your home and your workspace several times a day, using the preceding method (page 39)—call on the Light to breathe the negativity away from the room, all objects in the room, and yourself and release it to the earth for transmutation of this time.
- Thank the Light.
- Then call on the Light: *I call upon the Light, please veil this room/ house, all objects in this room/house, and myself with the highest positivity for the energy required of this day/night. I thank the Light.*

Always cleanse yourself and your space using the above alignment techniques *before* and *after* every healing session.

Cleanse your crystals *before* and *after* each healing session: in water; via an energy cleansing method; hands-on (only do this if you are very aligned and a competent practitioner).

Personal use of crystals

Simply being around crystals will energize you and help you to feel better. After you have meditated with crystals, or used crystals for healing on yourself or a member of the family, it is a good idea to get into water following the session. Bathe if you are able to, or take a shower. Being in water will help to align you and make you feel greatly refreshed, awake and aware.

Taking a crystal treatment

What can you expect if you visit a crystal therapist for crystal healing? Usually the sessions are very relaxing, once the crystals are placed on or around the body in whatever crystal configuration you require. Prior to the session, the crystal healer may ask you about any condition with which you may have presented. For example, if you have attended with a pain in your elbow, you might wish to outline the history of this injury; in the discussion on your elbow, your energy heightens, which is very good preparation for the crystals to "vacuum up" the cloud of negativity held in the energy field around the site of the elbow, when the crystals are in place and ignited to begin their work. The crystals will also pulse out a high charge of positive energy to the site of injury. I always ask clients to imagine that the negativity held in the energy field looks something like one of those metallic wiry pan scrubbers, like a cloud that is a collection of negativity in the energy field, above the site of injury or pain.

As the crystals begin to work, this cloud of negativity begins to thin and separate out, then dissipate as the crystal absorbs, over subsequent sessions, more and more of the cloud of dis-ease in the energy field, which has become something that has tracked from the energy field into the body. You may have this because it is a "samskara" or past-life wound, or you may have this because you have a weakness in your energy field—if it is your elbow, perhaps your energy is trying to tell you that you are inflexible. It may take more than one session to release the difficulty, but remember, it could have taken you many, many lives to accumulate it in the first place, so a degree of patience is required. We live in such a quick-fix, drug-dominant culture that we have become ingrained to expect instant results by popping a pill. To rebalance the energy field and, in turn, the physical body, we need to rethink our commitment to our own health and well-being.

Following the session of crystal healing, you may feel "spacey." This is because your energy field has probably expanded out several feet beyond the arm's length from the body at which it usually sits. Alignments from the therapist will bring your energy back in toward your body. Try not to, say, bend over to put on your shoes, as you may feel "swimmy", but instead move slowly and in a considered way until you have had a drink of water or herbal tea and perhaps a little something to eat. The reason eating or drinking helps is that your physical body has to function in processing the food and drink, so the body naturally working means its focus pulls the energy field, now cleaner and clearer, back to its resident natural state, no longer out around the room, but back at arm's length around the body. (Remember, it is very helpful to get into water by bathing following a crystal therapy session as this completes the rebalancing of the energy field following the expansion of energy that takes place during the session.)

When you feel completely happy that you are awake and aware, only then can you consider driving home. If you do not feel awake and aware, your crystal therapist will realign you further by working through the bands of your energy field with their hands until you are aligned fully.

Programming crystals

Programming crystals was a natural and daily occurrence in the advanced civilization of Atlantis. With their more enhanced Light-filled bodies, their greater connection to spiritual potential, their greater attunement to the energy of all around them, and the energetic manifestations of the Earth on which they stood, Atlantis was a Light- embodied civilization.

What does "programming" or "igniting" crystals mean?

Personal use

If you are intending to work with crystals at home, on yourself and the family around you, and not in a professional capacity, remember that simply holding your crystal and "asking," by using one of the recommended programs, is asking the Light/earth energies to empower your crystal. This means your crystal is charged with Light;

it is ignited for your use. You would then use the crystals you have asked to help you and when you have completed your session you would place those crystals immediately in water. This turns off the crystal ignition/charge as well as cleansing the crystals.

Prepare yourself to work with crystals in the following way:

Always cleanse your crystal first before programming and again after use. (See the section on cleansing crystals, page 21.)

Always hold the crystal in the right palm or place the right palm over the crystal for programming.

Professional use

If you are a professional crystal therapist, you would ask/program your crystals for your client, spend some time intuiting the client's energy field, then lay appropriate crystals on or around the client and ignite them (see Programming crystals, page 42) Following the appropriate healing time, you would then ask the Light that the crystals are turned off, carefully remove them, cleanse and align them, then align your client back to an "awake and aware" position and complete the follow-up on what the client experienced during the session, making sure the client is awake and aware enough to leave the therapy room and drive home.

Crystal circuitry

A professional crystal therapist will usually employ a method of crystal healing known as "crystal circuitry." This is where a kind of energy circuit is set up, rather like an electrical circuit, in that there is a "charge" crystal called an "ignitor" crystal and a "receiving" crystal called an "exit" crystal. Usually the ignitor crystal is placed above the crown of the head, appropriate to the circuit employed, and the exit crystal is placed appropriately in the energy field below the feet. The crystal therapist then places a configuration of crystals on the body/chakra points, as befits the requirements of the client, in

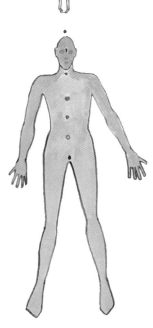

between the ignitor and exit crystals. The therapist ignites the crystals using a professional method of charge, a hands-on technique that works at a higher level for the client because the therapist is a "Lightworker." The therapist monitors the session and timing and then closes the energy of the crystals at the required time and removes them in a "Light-appropriate" way, aligning and settling the expanded energy of the client so that they return to an "awake and aware" state (this may require many alignments, followed by something to eat/drink in order that the client is fit to safely step back out into the world and drive home). Then the therapist cleanses and realigns the crystals, the healing space and themselves in readiness for the next client.

I have tried here to outline clearly how the responsibilities of a professional crystal therapist differ from the way in which we employ crystals in our everyday personal use.

Healing clients with crystals as a professional Lightworker carries greater energetic responsibility.

- Always align yourself and your space prior to and after crystal healing yourself or another.
- Always cleanse your crystal first before programming and again after use.
- Always hold the crystal in the right palm or place the right palm over the crystal for programming.
- Always use the full name of the client when programming crystals for their healing.

At the end of each of the eight crystal chapters is a list with a number of ideas for crystal healing. Further suggestions for the many ways in which crystals can help you in your everyday life are listed in the A–Z of Important Crystals at the end of the book. Simply use any of the four "templates" featured here to create your own crystal program, tailored to your own individual crystal healing requirements. Programmed crystals can be worn or carried, placed beside or beneath the bed at night for personal use, and for therapy use crystals can be incorporated into crystal circuitry.

Templates for creating your own crystal program

• **Personal use: to veil positive energy**

I ask the Light [or earth energies] to please charge this crystal to veil [full name] with healing for [healing focus]. Thank you.

• **Personal use: to absorb negative energy**

I ask the Light [or earth energies] to please charge this crystal to release from [full name] the negative holding of energy of [healing focus, such as blocked tear ducts] that [full name] may move forward in greater positive energetic flow. Thank you.

• **Therapy use:to veil positive energy**

I call upon the Light, please charge this crystal with the highest positivity to veil [full name] with the Light of/for [healing focus]. I thank the Light.

• **Therapy use: to absorb negative energy**

I call upon the Light, please charge this crystal to release all the negative energy from [full name] to veil the highest positivity of [healing focus, for example the Light of peace] to their difficulty with [healing challenge, for example anger issues] that [full name] may move forward in greater Light alignment and positive, harmonious energetic flow. I thank the Light.

Crystal toolkit

A crystal home toolkit should consist of:
Rose quartz
Amethyst
Pyrite
Celestite
Smoky quartz
Citrine
Fluorite
Unakite

These are the eight basic minimum crystal types that I would ask you to have and to use at home. As we look at each crystal, with information that only very briefly describes their incredible individual capacity to bring great joy and benefit to your life and your health, please remember that vast volumes could be written on every crystal, but I seek to outline some basic and simple uses which you can happily and confidently begin at home.

Although I describe a selection of eight crystals with which to start your kit, you will require several pieces of each crystal listed. You will need many pieces of rose quartz in different shapes and sizes, several amethysts of different shapes and sizes, and so on, throughout the whole list. This is because shape and sizes does make a difference (if only in the crystal world). Shape denotes whether the crystal has the capacity to "point" energy in a focused way or to "hum out" energy in an even way, mirroring its shape; some crystals can do both. Size is not an issue when it comes to the capacity of magnification of energy, but it is an issue when it comes to the absorption of negative energy. For example, if you live near a pylon or a telecommunications mast then you are living near a very negative magnetic energy emission source and are constantly being *severely* energy challenged.

This can be alleviated and in some cases almost totally eradicated by the use of crystals and I urge you to do something immediately if you are in this position at home, work, or school. Pyrite (see page 73) can carry out this negative energy absorption highly effectively. The rule of thumb is that you need an adequate amount of pyrite energy to tackle this demanding job—meeting and absorbing the negative energy emissions of the pylon/mast. For this, your small, appliance-size, pyrite "cube" would not work (it would be at saturation level very quickly), but a lump or rounded piece, approximately the size of a man's rounded fist, programmed to absorb this negative energy and return it to the earth for transmutation would do just that *in perpetuity* if programmed to do so, and if left within 12 feet (3.5m) of the pylon/mast outside or planted 3 feet (1m) into the earth.

So simple, yet why are we not taking this responsibility to heal and care for ourselves and others? I know many wonderful people who visit such sites and "crystal plant" pyrite. The advantage of crystal planting is that the crystal is not disturbed or handled. You really would *not* want to have to deal with any crystal in this capacity once it starts working in this way, nor would you want anyone to accidentally pick up a pyrite that was working so hard, absorbing the quantity of negative electromagnetic emissions that pour off a pylon. The pyrite would be working hard and would feel very uncomfortable to the touch, particularly if you are energy-sensitive.

I have described the use of pyrite to illustrate an example of the importance of the shape of a crystal. The diagrams on this page show crystals and their energy emissions and will help you to focus on what the crystals are doing as you begin to work with them.

A crystal that "points" energy

A crystal that "hums" energy

Rose quartz

Healing qualities:

Peace

Promotes healing

Heals skin

Heals pain

Effuses the energy of love from the heart

Calms emotional upset

Promotes peaceful relationships

Actively seeks to heal

Rose quartz is, in truth, one of the greatest holistic healing gifts this planet has ever seen. If only more people were open to its properties and uses, their lives would be enhanced in ways beyond their imagining. I have listed above just a few key properties of a rose quartz, and in the following pages I shall briefly outline some of the ways (and these are infinitesimal) you may use rose quartz for yourself and in your home.

The rose quartz "Heart of Light"

I cannot move on without mentioning the rose quartz "heart of Light." You may have seen crystal hearts in your local crystal shop: smooth, shaped crystals that are lovely to hold and have around. Some years ago, a group of healers with a particular soul connection received a dispensation of Light that allowed them to program some of these hearts—in rose quartz only—to ignite them with healing energy to help people connect to "Christ Consciousness." Christ Consciousness is about the pure divine you, the *you* that you have always wanted to be, whole and pure, giving of heart, making choices from the heart in alignment to the divine plan and your soul purpose in service to *your* soul and not your ego or lower self. Christ Consciousness came about through the highest gift that Master Jesus blessed to our planet Earth through his example. If we live in likeness to this, then we shall ascend from the wheel of rebirth to live in Light, no longer needing to incarnate on to the dense realms of Earth, yet to work in Light, further developing on our "soul journey." You may or may not believe and accept that you are on a soul journey, or that you are a soul who inhabits a physical body at this time. If this is news to you, I hope you will be open-hearted and minded; however, I do not feel it is my role to convince you, as belief and faith are personal choices and exploring your soul opportunities is a personal development issue.

These rose quartz hearts of Light are charged and ignited by Light-workers, who energy cleanse and invest them with Light energy. Upon receipt, hold the rose quartz heart in your right hand for five minutes, during which time the crystal ignites to your own energy imprint and requirements (remember, the energy of the crystal immediately meets and seeks to balance your energy). Then you may carry the crystal, meditate with it, and put it under your pillow when you sleep, to enhance your peace and your soul/divine connection to Light.

Rose quartz heart of Light at the end of life

I would highly recommend you try a rose quartz heart, which has all the properties of rose quartz and greater power enhancement beyond. They are also great gifts to give to those you love and care about or who are in pain or stress.

For example, a few years ago a dear friend was diagnosed with an aggressive cancer and I took her a rose quartz heart of Light. She was a little skeptical, feeling quite desperate in her pain and shock at the discovery of her illness; great fear had consumed her, for herself, for her partner and her young children, and her wider family; she was a strong person and many around her sought her strength to add to their own.

All through her illness, her tests, and her very unpleasant treatment, she carried her heart of Light. She held it in her hand tightly when she had her long body scan and during those times felt great peace and stillness and as if she were being "held" in Light. She often placed the rose quartz directly onto the point of pain and felt great relief and renewed strength to cope. I often helped her and cleansed her crystals for her and I never ceased to be amazed at how hard the crystals worked. Her rose quartz, which she wore constantly, together with her heart of Light rose quartz, which she kept near her to hold, both developed a cloudy grey tinge through use and yet when cleansed and refreshed they returned to a vibrant, clean, pink glow.

My friend passed to the Light. She was brave, beautiful, and, I am sure, more prepared and spiritually connected than she would have been had she not accepted the gift of the rose quartz.

There are many things you can do with crystals to help the long-term sick and terminally ill. There are both basic and advanced courses available that you can seek out. If you have an interest in this area, ask the Light to help you connect to the most appropriate course/group for you.

Rose quartz heart for pain relief

I will share another intriguing story with you to illustrate the power of the rose quartz and in particular the rose quartz heart of Light.

My husband had a dreadful accident some years ago, incurring life-changing injuries that have left him in constant pain. Apart from meditation and holistic therapy, which give him some brief respite from his plight (receiving pain in this way from a soul perspective can be a way a person chooses to clear karma), crystals have helped him immensely, and those of us around him to cope with his very difficult day-to-day experience of living with such a high degree of pain.

Through this challenging experience, over a considerable length of time, we have learned a great deal about crystal use to help relieve pain. One crystal of great benefit for pain on whatever level, be it physical, emotional, mental, or spiritual, is the humble rose quartz.

Some years ago, we were on holiday in the UK, in Cornwall, and my husband was particularly unwell, suffering with ill health and severe pain. He had a rose quartz heart of Light, along with other crystals, and we had done considerable energetic work to help to alleviate his greatest discomfort in the hope that he would get some sleep. I often hold my rose quartz heart of Light at night, both to help me sleep and to enhance my connection to Light. On this occasion, I had fallen asleep with my rose quartz heart of Light in my hand, while my husband had his beneath his pillow to help him relax, to overcome the extremity of the pain, and to attempt to get some quality rest.

On this particular holiday, we were in a quaint old cottage and the beds were all single. I slept peacefully and awoke the next morning to find my rose quartz heart of Light missing, only to discover it across the bedroom on the floor, directly beneath the point of the greatest pain my husband was experiencing in his spine. His own rose quartz heart of Light had moved from beneath his pillow to his tummy, again in direct line with the pain in his spine, but at the front of his body.

I understand how crystals work, yet what had happened still amazed me. Crystals work by magnetic energy attraction and they magnetize to healing opportunities. My husband's own crystal had magnetized to his pain (front) and my rose quartz had quite literally journeyed from my relaxed hand, many feet away from him, and situated itself on the floor beneath him, yet at the nearest point to assuage the pain in his spine.

My husband describes his experience of the use of crystals, with regards to the pain he endures, as "taking the edge off." He feels he has the energy capacity better to cope with and manage living with pain as a result of using crystals alongside his prescribed medications and physio treatments. He feels the inner strengthening quality of the crystals also really helps him cope.

Rose quartz heart for changing your "energy"

I have received some uplifting letters from people who have also had amazing results with their own rose quartz hearts of Light.

One letter was from an eight-year-old girl whose mother purchased a rose quartz heart of Light for her because she was being bullied. The little girl carried it and said she immediately felt a sense of peace—no longer fearful. It charged her energy, she no longer seemed magnetized to her situations of fear, and the bullying stopped. (Consider this: if someone's energy field changes, then the energy around them changes also. For this little girl, something in her energy field shifted, her energy strengthened, and in that alchemical movement of energy the people who challenged her so negatively moved on, focusing away from choosing to pick on her.)

In her letter, she wrote a thank you for her *Christal* and I felt she was perfectly in tune with the divine energy flow from the crystal and had empowered herself to her own "Christ Consciousness." I felt her spelling of the word was a delightful sign and I hope you feel a similar connection to this wonderful rose quartz, strong enough to get one for yourself.

Carry a rose quartz

Some male clients balk a little at wearing a rose quartz over their heart chakra. If they do feel reluctant, then it is not a problem; it is sufficient to carry rose quartz in a small pouch (the pouch is important to help hold purification to the energy emitted)—a midnight blue velvet pouch, for example, is very good. Pockets are negative "soup" areas; money, keys, and heaven-knows-what-else your men friends may have in their pockets all carry an imprint of negative energy. (Handbags/purses are the same.) It is possible to energy cleanse your money, keys and so on; however, a rose quartz or other crystal carried for healing purposes in a pouch will hold its power of healing vibration for longer.

Crystals to be carried in a pocket/pouch must be cleansed before and after use, so before you put on your clothes in the morning, cleanse and ask your crystal for the energy you require (for example, hold the crystal in your right palm and ask *that the rose quartz veil you with the light of peace and beauty and unconditional love in all that you do, all that you think, all that you say, for that day*). Then place the crystal in a pouch and secure the pouch in your pocket. Always have some safety pins handy as you will be amazed at how many garments have no pockets. You can also pin the pouch to the waist of a dress or jacket and some people even pin their crystal pouches inside their underwear. Do whatever you find most comfortable.

After use, say at the end of the day, wash your crystal in clear cold water and place it in a glass bowl/dish in the moonlight overnight, to rest the crystal and replenish its energy.

Then repeat the asking of the crystal in the morning when you get dressed again, and so on. Try it and you will see huge differences to your life. I have known people with great challenges to their life and energy—great fear, great pain, you name it—and they have sustained greater peace and connectedness and open-heartedness, greater alignment to their heart plan, their divine soul mission, all through the use of the rose quartz. This method is very simple to achieve and I urge you to give it a try.

Rose quartz meditation

The rose quartz heart of Light is a wonderful meditational tool. Lay it on the heart chakra or sit and hold the crystal in your right palm. The rose quartz heart of Light will aid sleep and bring peace to fraught moments. Place it beneath the pillow or hold it in your right palm and feel yourself breathe in your energy of peace emitted from the crystal.

A piece of rose quartz can enhance your capacity to increase your vibrational rate through meditation, which in turn helps you to go beyond the mind to higher and higher levels of consciousness. Some people sit with masters in the Light, others go "off" and remember nothing, yet feel a rejuvenation of energy, a sense of peace and well-being that increases with daily practice. A useful thing to remember is to let go of the notion of "connecting" with any sense of expectation. Meditation takes on different qualities at different times and is a very personal journey. I have found it helpful to remember that each time I sit down to meditate I am stopping still to allow the Light to catch me, to fill me, to enfold me. It is a measure of how much you respect yourself and your energy field and of how much you love yourself to give yourself the time to simply sit still and catch the Light. Remember, when you stop and catch the Light your energy field will become bigger, stronger, and more enhanced; you will have a greater sense of self-empowerment and a greater capacity to ground and action your intuition, your "inner tuition," which is your Light-guided inspiration.

Rose quartz to aid peaceful sleep

A hyperactive child I know, who was recommended a rose quartz heart of Light to wear pinned on his clothes and to place under his pillow at night, experienced a very noticeable change: he slept! This was unheard of previously. He had not slept a full night in longer than his parents could remember, which meant, of course, that they had not slept either. Any piece of rose quartz can be programmed to enhance restful, peaceful sleep.

Sleep is interesting. I have first-hand experience of how tiring and frustrating it can be if your children do not sleep. No one is at their best in this kind of energy; however, sleep is not always optimum rest. I also know a great many people who sleep and sleep, yet do not awaken refreshed, rested, and energized. I know from my own experience that when I, or others around me, find an inability to sleep, regular, even short, meditations provide a great energy boost and feeling of alignment, together with a sense of balance to enable you to "get through," things you would not think you could achieve on no sleep. I would encourage any insomniacs to meditate as there are many bonuses; however, the one that may interest insomniacs the most is that if you are in greater balance and harmony energetically, you will find you are able to sleep better.

Crystal portals

This sounds very "Stargate," doesn't it! Lots of people like the idea of a crystal portal to use as a meditation tool and of course, that is very possible and many crystals can help you in that way. However, I refer here to a more earthly portal.

It is possible to energy cleanse everyone that comes into your home with crystal energy by creating a "portal of Light" at the doors, in and out, of your home. That way, people are cleansed of their energetic "rubbish" and enter your home in greater peace, alignment, balance, and harmony, and they walk around in your home in a beautiful veil of peace, Light, and harmony. Upon leaving your home, they are again washed with peace, Light, and harmony.

Pause a moment and consider the potentials for this. How many times do you charge in from work carrying the energetic rubbish of the day? Does this affect your partner? Does this affect your kids? Does this ruin your evening? Of course! And your partner and kids will have all sorts of energy challenges to deal with. Perhaps your husband/partner works with computers and has a bad journey home in the car, or on the train. Imagine the awful energy you travel in or work in. Don't you want to take that off before you come home? Don't you wish your home to be a place of peace, a sanctuary of harmony and energy replenishment for all who come within? By using crystals, it can be.

To create a portal of energy, to veil peace to all who come within your home, you simply have to place rose quartz (tiny tumbled pieces will suffice) at the corners of your door. Attach the rose quartz with some adhesive putty if there is no framework to rest it on. To attach crystals to the lower corners, try using low-tack adhesive (I have lost many a crystal inadvertently in the vacuum cleaner when I have used small ones placed on the floor, so I now favor larger ornamental pieces; however, the small ones work just as well).

Before placing your rose quartz around the door, hold the stones in your right palm (after cleansing first) and ask *that they veil your home and all who come within your home with the Light of peace, love, and harmony, and all who leave with the blessings of love.*

Another amazing advantage of creating a portal of crystal Light at the entrance to your home is the mail! The mail you receive carries energy you simply would not believe. Think of the awful offices and computers that produce your correspondence, your bills, your junk mail. It does not bear thinking about, never mind the other letters that you receive; they, too, carry the energy of the sender and all those who have had contact with your mail on its journey to you.

If your mailbox is in your door and you have set up a crystal portal, your mail quite literally receives an energy cleanse as it passes through and lands on your mat. If you have an external mailbox, place a rose quartz within it and an amethyst to either side on the ground (you may plant them), so that your mail is cleansed and made positive.

As we have already seen, outside "planted" crystals need no cleansing as the elements take care of that. However, your "mailbox" rose quartz needs to be cleansed weekly, overnight in water.

Crystals and bathing

I have been asked about crystal portals in other areas of the home. Many people like the idea of a crystal portal in their bathroom, for example. If this idea appeals, place a citrine at each side of the top of the bathroom door, on the bathroom side, and an amethyst either side of the bases of the door. Cleanse the stones prior to placing and then hold them in your right palm and ask *that these crystals cleanse and purify your four lower bodies and the four lower bodies of all who enter this space, that all negativity be absorbed by the crystals and released to the earth for transmutation, and that positivity, harmony, balance and alignment, peace, and great joy fill and enfold you as you move beyond this space and go forward veiled in Light energy.*

Do not be tempted to place crystal configurations around the bath. It is not a good idea nowadays in modern homes, as baths are normally in close proximity to toilets, tanks, plumbing, and chemicals. Need I go on? In ancient times sacred pools were jewel-filled and of high energy, and they were cared for and protected by those charged with high knowledge and attainment with regard to crystals. If you like the idea of crystal bathing, then a good way to do that now, happily and positively, is to introduce "gem remedies" to your bath.

Remember, bathing is a key and important element of crystal healing. Bathing realigns the human energy field, as we are made up of so much water. Our molecular structure responds to being in water and to water (intake) replenishment. Working with crystals, you will find you are increasingly thirsty (drink lots of spring water).

If you do not have a bath, worry not. Create a crystal shower. Take a cheesecloth, about 12 inches (30cm) square in size, and in the center of the cloth place four rose quartz and two amethyst (tiny tumbled pieces will do). The amethyst will cleanse your four lower bodies and the rose quartz will veil you with the energy of peace and positivity. Stitch the cloth containing the crystals into a closed pouch, and tie the pouch onto your shower head. If it is a power shower, make sure you have a sturdy attachment.

This should not be confused with crystal configuration work, as these crystals for the shower will work more gently and effuse a wonderful energy over you, together with the shower water, a cleansing and positivizing energy veil.

Rose quartz to create a peaceful home and garden

To bring a veil of peace to your home and garden, or other environment, create a crystal "cairn." Cairns are ancient stone mounds; all over the world there are still cairns in existence that were put together many hundreds of years ago.

Get some positive, quality stones or pebbles and place them in a mound shape, making sure you site your cairn in a free-flowing place in your garden (I have even seen them on patios/verandahs/porches). By "free-flowing," I mean with air circulating around them and not, say, by a stagnant pond or overgrown area. Choose an area that will receive wind, light, and rain. Then place on the top of the cairn a large lump/rock of rose quartz. Ask that the rose quartz (if too big to hold, place your right hand over the stone) *veil your home, your land, your neighborhood, your community, with the Light of great peace and positivity and positive energy flow.* Then happily leave your rose quartz to do its work on your behalf. It will self-cleanse in the elements and you may notice greater enhancement to your plants, flowers, and trees, not to mention attracting wildlife to your garden.

Ask your "home" crystals to help you. If you have a rose quartz in your living room and you know and understand rose quartz is for "peace" and "harmony" and to promote "unconditional love"—well, we could all do with a bit of that, couldn't we? Why not let yourself and all the others who visit your home, your family and friends, receive that positive energy vibration also. Simply wash your lump of rose quartz by placing it in a bowl of water overnight, then pat dry with a natural cloth and, if you can hold it, program as below. If it is too large or cumbersome, place your right hand or both hands onto its surface, then ask *that the Light [or the Earth energy, if you prefer] veil my home, and all those who come within my home, with the beauty of peace, Light, harmony, and unconditional love—thank you.*

A note about "who" exactly it is that you are asking when you program/ask to charge your crystals. You are making an invocation to the Light/the universe/ the Earth energy, whichever higher power you are most comfortable with attuning to.

Perform this cleansing and programming weekly, unless your home or family is experiencing some kind of difficulty or an emotionally challenging time, in which case cleanse and ask for the help of the crystal more frequently. Then observe the results. You will experience and, if you are intuitive, "see" a difference in those within your home, and those who visit will receive a wash of peace and Light from your beautiful rose quartz, whom you have called into service. It is a beautiful thing to do for yourself and for others. How many people can say, "Well, today I went to a friend's house and I received a gift of Light, a healing, a veil of peace, and a gift of the energy of unconditional love"? That is just what a visitor to your home may say if you work with your rose quartz to greater facilitate its Light and beauty.

These are just a few of the many thousands of things you can do with a rose quartz. Try them yourself and I am sure you will soon receive amazing results, together with a greater positive enhancement to your life.

Programming rose quartz

See page 42 for more information on how to program crystals.

For personal use

I ask the Light [or earth energies] to please charge this crystal to veil [full name] with healing for [healing focus]. Thank you.

For professional use

I call upon the Light, please charge this crystal with the highest positivity to veil [full name] with the Light of/for [healing focus]. I thank the Light.

Examples of healing focus:
- Promoting the energy of peace
- Unconditional love
- Promoting general healing
- Veiling the energy of peace to pain
- Promoting specific healing to [name area of the body]
- A "portal of peace"
- Energy cleansing (shower bag)
- Peace (for a cairn)
- Healing a "sore" on the earth
- Peace, harmony, and positive flow (car)
- Wounds/scars/skin healing

Amethyst

Healing qualities:

Emotional cleanser

Absorbs negative energy

Absorbs negative emotional energy

The stone of transmutation

Environmental cleanser

Strengthens spiritual connection

Enhances connection to nature spirits, devas and elementals, faeries

Beacon of connection to other planetary activity

There has never been a time on our planet when we have been more in need of the purifying, transmutational qualities that emanate from amethyst. Whether we use amethyst to cleanse our own four lower bodies, to improve the energy of others, or the environment around us, amethyst can help better our health and well-being in so many ways.

You may wish to create a garden "cairn" (see section on rose quartz, page 59) with an amethyst on the top and ask that the crystal amethyst cleanse and purify your environment, that it be charged with high positivity and spiritual connection.

I know people who have done this, who meditate regularly with their amethyst cairns, and what they all have in common is that with regular and sustained meditation the Light enhancement of the cairn grows; some of those people have used this energy boost to "travel" galactically and connect to other "planetary consciousness." Also, the greater the purity of the garden, the more likely you will be to attract "nature spirits," who have been dealt a heavy blow by the profanity of our planet, together with man's lack of respect for the Earth and for the other natural life forms that inhabit our planet. I know many people seek greater connection to this stream of consciousness—Earth and nature spirits—as well as to the streams of consciousness of other planets. The amethyst cairn will be a great tool to help you to be successful with this goal.

Wearing amethyst

We have already discussed amethyst in the form of a "bed" for cleansing your crystals. We have also outlined how you may use amethyst tumbled pieces as part of a cleansing portal, which will cleanse the energy of any being who passes through that veil of transmutational crystal energy.

If you wear amethyst over your heart chakra or, even better, on a longer cord or chain over your solar plexus chakra, you will have a great opportunity to release much negative emotional holding and realign your newly cleansed chakras to be able to breathe in with greater purity the positivity of the universal energy.

I have included, below, some drawings of a client with an emotional difficulty. Here, a relationship of many years ended abruptly and this particular client felt great loss, hurt, and abandonment. She was unwilling to face her future and was heavily dependent on her partner. She was in a state of constant emotional turmoil and was struggling to overcome the break-up or find any positive thing to live for.

As well as receiving other healing (reflexology, soul counseling and life plan work, regular alignments), she was asked to wear, over a period of eight weeks, an amethyst crystal every other day and a rose quartz crystal in between. The amethyst was to be worn over the solar plexus chakra and the rose quartz over the heart chakra.

| *The chakras of a client with emotional difficulty before crystal use* | *After four weeks of wearing alternate crystals—rose quartz and amethyst* | *After eight weeks of wearing rose quartz and amethyst* |

The first illustration shows the negative thought processing around her head in the form of a dark cloud of energy. Her throat chakra is blocked, indicating that she has difficulty expressing herself, and her heart chakra is working but has dark plumes around it, signifying she is disheartened. The plumes of negative energy on her solar plexus chakra show she has emotional trauma, which is giving her stomach problems. Her knees and ankles have energy blocks, which denote she feels she cannot move forward in future.

You can see from the illustrations that after four weeks of wearing the crystals, the negative energy plumes are receding. Her solar plexus chakra has calmed down, her heart chakra is functioning more freely, her block to the throat chakra is reducing, and the energy around her head looks better as she begins to feel she can see light at the end of the tunnel.

After eight weeks, you can see her energy field is expanded, giving her more hope. There is a significant change to her mental energy, she does not feel as burdened, the emotional trauma is reducing, her throat chakra is beginning to open, and her heart chakra is more open and flowing, with the result that the energy field as a whole is beginning to function properly. Note the reduction of negative energy around the stomach, knees, and ankles; although crystals were not used on these areas, moving the negative energy of emotional trauma has moved this stuck energy too.

Asking clients to wear crystals to heal themselves is a common part of the "homework" that crystal therapists can give to clients. Remember, no therapist will ever heal you or anyone else; a good therapist may, however, facilitate you to heal yourself.

Life is, among other things, about personal responsibility and only you can change your life. The amethyst crystal helped to absorb the client's highly negative feelings and to ease her considerable emotional pain; the rose quartz helped to wash her energy field with a high charge of the vibration of peace. After wearing these crystals, alternately, for a week, she felt calmer, more accepting of her situation. She was able to sleep better, she was less angry, and was beginning to respond to the understanding, although she was not yet happy about it, that her soul was offering her a fantastic learning opportunity in her new-found freedom.

Amethyst as a cleansing protector

Imagine for a moment that you live in a very run-down area; crime there is high and there are unsavory characters all around you. You may feel your land or your home is tainted by something negative, or persons who are negative. It is a challenging and unhappy position to be in—yet in many areas, perhaps in inner cities, an all too common one.

Some years ago, a group of therapist friends and I worked in a very depressed area and shared a therapy center there. We were learning and experiencing at first hand our newfound but in fact very ancient wisdom that is the knowledge of crystals. We had been broken into on several occasions and were growing despondent at our efforts to maintain a sanctuary of high positivity for the community to share in. At times, we felt more than a little overwhelmed by events on our doorstep, which were so cruel and negative.

Crystals are a great help for these types of situations. You can plant amethyst in the far corners of your land as boundary stones and ask that they create an "energy perimeter" to your personal environment (your garden and your home, for example) that protects the positive energy within the energy perimeter from the negativity without. Once you have charged the crystals with this task and then planted them, walk the perimeter, if that is possible, in a clockwise circuit three times around, imagining that you are winding a violet Light from crystal to crystal as you go. All within the perimeter energy fence of amethyst Light is violet Light and therefore transmuting of negativity, in turn protecting you from the energy from beyond that Light fence.

For people to accept the real and powerful role that energy plays in all things, I would urge you to look at energy pictures. Look at heat emissions from the Earth, look at energy photographs of the body, that show "dis-ease" in the energy field. It is possible to record energy emissions and this is a common everyday occurrence in many orthodox fields of work, such as engineering, medicine, and meteorology. Energy is everything and when we deny its effects we work against the natural laws of energy, against the natural laws of the universe. To a skeptic, I would say: try crystals, you have nothing to lose by having a go, at say, amethyst planting the perimeters of your garden. You may surprise yourself, if you have an open mind and an open heart. More than that, you may gain great enhancement to your life and help positivize your surroundings.

Amethyst to strengthen spiritual connection

For this purpose, amethyst may be used in many ways. Your crystal therapist may, for example, choose to work with you using an amethyst "chrysanthemum," which, if placed above your crown chakra during healing (for no more than five to ten minutes), accelerates and opens the aperture of the crown chakra to draw within that chakra a greater Light quotient. With this enhanced increment of Light drawn into your being, together with an open and free-flowing crown chakra, you can draw in greater strength and alignment, as well as greater attunement to your divine plan.

I would not recommend trying an amethyst chrysanthemum session without the assistance of a competent crystal healer. For personal use, to promote and strengthen your spiritual connection, first take a rounded, tumbled piece of amethyst and hold it in the palm of your right hand (remember "right to receive, left to leave" is something of a rule in energy terms), then ask *that the amethyst facilitate your greater connection to Spirit in all that you can achieve in connection to the divine will of the soul.*

Then meditate with the crystal amethyst in your right palm for 10–20 minutes only.

Some people struggle with the concept of time in meditation and wish to "go off" for as long as possible, but this is not necessary. Better to meditate and to connect to Spirit little and often—at least twice a day, even if it is only for 5–10 minutes. With practice this is easy to achieve, giving you points of recharge and realignment to divine consciousness and the will of the soul. You can make this a key part of your routine, like visiting the bathroom, brushing your teeth, and getting dressed. I usually remind people that they would not venture out of the house naked, yet why would anyone choose to go out into the world with their energy unaligned and unprotected, unclothed by the Light, which is there to be readily and rightfully called on to align and protect you, which will fill and enfold you with great positive energy, ready to meet any and every new challenge.

Amethyst: the stone of transmutation

Violet as a color is a powerful visualization method to release negative holding. Color visualization for meditation and healing should not be underestimated. Wearing color for healing is also an important healing complement. For example, wear violet if you have a "cold"—a cold is a manifestation of a release of negativity, often emotional, and wearing the color violet promotes and enhances that color vibration in your own energy field and therefore helps you move through the process more quickly. If you struggle to visualize color, place a scarf or piece of card in the correct color on your wall and then focus on it, imagining that you are breathing in that color as you go into a meditation.

There are many beautiful violet crystals and many that will help you to release and transmute negative holding. Amethyst, however, is the primary choice for transmutation.

Let's say I have a stomach virus or influenza. I am feeling very unwell, low in energy, and it is all I can do to sit up in bed. To help someone with such an illness, place an amethyst under the bed, near the center of the floor beneath it, but before doing so, charge the crystal by asking (by holding the crystal in your right palm) *that the amethyst absorb all negative energy and encourage a cleansing of the four lower bodies of [say the person's full name here].*

When you place the crystal under the bed the person moves more quickly through the release of the illness. They should also take lots of baths, if they can, while the person caring for them should remember to cleanse the used crystal often in water. It would be best to rotate two amethyst crystals every 12 hours (one under the bed for 12 hours, then in water for 12 hours, and an alternate "active" amethyst in place under the bed charged to heal the sick person.)

Let's say I suffer from stress and worry at work and as a result have a feeling of general debilitation. I am not ill but I do not feel well. A good way of alleviating this feeling would be to sit on the floor, cross-legged if possible and with a straight back, or if not then on a chair with your feet placed flat on the floor, shoulder-width apart. Then take two double-terminated amethyst points and lay one across each palm, in a line pointing down toward the middle finger and up toward the forearm. Leave the crystals in place for 10 minutes. Having previously cleansed the crystal points, ask *that the crystals absorb any negativity in the body and energy field,* asking *that the crystals, in turn, charge [full name] with the veil of the "Light of transmutation" in order that [full name] may transmute their negative energy and be replenished with Light and positivity in its place.*

Repeat weekly, if necessary, and you will be amazed at the results. After use, place the amethyst points in water overnight in order to cleanse them immediately following the session.

Programming amethyst

See page 42 for more information on how to program crystals.

For personal use

I ask the Light [or earth energies] to please charge this crystal to veil [full name] with healing for [healing focus]. Thank you.

For professional use

I call upon the Light, please charge this crystal with the highest positivity to veil to [full name] with the Light of/for [healing focus]. I thank the Light.

Examples of healing focus:
- Personal purification and transmutation
- Crystal shower (in conjunction with rose quartz)
- Cairn for environmental cleansing
- Cairn for spiritual connection
- To release held emotional negativity
- To create a boundary of Light protection
- To facilitate spiritual connection
- To help to overcome illness
- To help overcome stress and debilitation

Pyrite

Healing qualities:

Absorbs negative electromagnetic energy from:

Household kitchen appliances

Television

Computers

Cell phones

For personal healing:

Promotes release of stubborn
held negative energy patterning

Pyrite is an incredible gift to us at this time. We live on a planet that, through our own man-made destruction, is now awash with negative electromagnetic energy, and if we could actually see it, we would be truly horrified by the soup of negative energy that swirls around us constantly. It truly is everywhere—in our homes, our cars, our schools and offices, our hospitals, our cities, and our countryside.

I pondered hard on how best to present this information to make it easy for the reader, and feel the best way to approach this section on pyrite is to list everyday items and occurrences that are potentially harmful to us all, together with the energetic antidote as a follow-on.

Electrical appliances

Most electrical appliances give off baseline negative electromagnetic charge. One appliance in isolation (an oven or kettle, used several times a day) emits a negative charge as illustrated below. However, let's be honest, in most households we are all making merry with a number of appliances. Think of throwing in the toaster, microwave, juicer, food processor, washing machine, dryer, and dishwasher—all being switched on every day, some of them several times, and that is a lot of negative electromagnetic energy flying about.

This illustration shows the energy of the electrical forces when every-day kitchen appliances are operating. The stream of red running up the wall from the plug socket, for example, is the negative energy from the internal wiring, which will be running all around your house wherever you have such wiring. The blue in the electrical oven is the energy emitted from your food as it cooks, while the swirling red is the negative energy of the electrical charge from the fan-assisted oven. The most extreme appliance in the room is the microwave, illustrated to show the energy of frictional negative electric charge when the appliance is switched on. The washing machine is shown with the main charge coming from the control panel. The rim of the door and the outside of the machine are shown with the electric charge's negative energetic vibration in motion. The refrigerator shows the main negative energy coming from the back, which then envelops the appliance.

Looking carefully at the illustration of a typical kitchen with all the appliances switched on together, showing the emissions of negative electromagnetic energy emanating around the room from them, it is fortunate that we have the gift of pyrite, which has the capacity to absorb almost all the negative electromagnetic emissions around you. Please remember, your pyrite will be working very hard so the trick is to keep cleansing it very often.

To absorb negative electromagnetic energy emitted from appliances

1. Place a cleansed pyrite near each electric plug socket and ask *that the pyrite absorb all negative electromagnetic emissions given off by these connected appliances.* (Cleanse pyrite each week overnight in water.)
2. You can use one larger size (a fist-sized piece) pyrite on the windowsill (cleansed) and programmed by asking *that the pyrite absorb all negative electromagnetic emissions given off by all appliances in the room.* (Cleanse pyrite each week overnight in water.)

A note about microwaves

Microwaves are truly powerful generators of negative electromagnetic energy and if possible should not be housed in your kitchen. I know that sounds odd, but if you have to use a microwave try to place it in a utility space near the kitchen, or house it in a cupboard space to help contain its negative emissions.

Food should be energy cleansed as a matter of course, no matter how you cook and prepare it. If you do not do this currently, a good method is to call on the Light and ask *that your meal (and the food that you serve to others) is cleansed of all negative energy and in turn that negative energy is released to the earth for transmutation.* Then call to the Light again and ask *that your food be invested with the highest positive energy and nutritional value for your energy replenishment at this time.*

Food out of the microwave should be especially thoroughly energy cleansed. To help with the cleansing and absorption of the microwave negative emissions, place a pyrite on or near the microwave. Wash in water weekly, then replace the pyrite to continue its work in giving your environment greater purity.

Television

The television is another powerful emitter of negativity—one, because it is electrical and two, because it magnifies energy directly into our homes. For example, I prefer to watch programs about the animal kingdom, nature, places of interest, and comedy or inspirational programs. I don't like those with negativity, profanity, or violence, and the reason I don't like such negativity on my television is that I know that the energy of what I watch is projected into my home; it does not stay in the "box," but instead as an energy it comes right out into your living room, your kitchen, your bedroom, or wherever you watch television.

Having three children, I know how difficult it can be to monitor the amount of television that they want to, or actually do, watch. However, I do limit and monitor their viewing because I understand about energy and I know that my children engage their energy with television—as does anyone watching it—and it takes you into a state of brain sleep. Too much viewing and children cannot think, react, or function as they should.

In many homes, television is a great way to prevent conversation; it may be on all day and night and this is not good for you, even if you watch only banal programs such as soaps. I would say do not let your children watch very much television at all. Be choosy about what you and they watch. Consider the energy of what you view and, most importantly, learn to align yourself and your children after watching it. If your children play at gaming on your television set or on consoles, they are also taken further into a brain sleep state. Gaming, too, should be limited, and think hard about the quality of the energy of the game—how negative is it really? Always align your children after gaming.

To align your children after gaming or television

- Seat them before you.
- Hold your hands together in prayer and stand behind them.
- Ask them to close their eyes and quietly, or in your mind, ask *that all negativity may be released from them to the earth for transmutation and that the child may now be veiled in the Light of peace, harmony, and positivity.*
- Thank the Light for this help.

It takes seconds to perform this alignment technique, yet it makes a huge difference to the health and well-being of your child and the energy of your home. You will feel better because, even if you do not know and understand very much about energy, deep down you will intuitively understand and know in your heart that it is not good for you or your children to have the television on all day and night, or be gaming for hours and hours at a time. You will feel better for knowing that you have satisfied your own inner knowledge and inner wisdom.

To absorb negativity from a television

Place a cleansed pyrite on or behind the set and ask that the pyrite *absorb all negative emissions from that television facilitator and from any broadcast program, that your environment may be veiled with peace and purity.*

Cleanse the pyrite weekly overnight in water, well away from the television itself.

Computers

Most homes now have a variety of computers and laptops, perhaps even multiples of each. We have them at work, on the train, in the car; wherever we go now, we are bombarded by the waves of negative electromagnetic energy given off by a computer. The type of energy given off affects in particular our mental energy and I feel we shall see, in time, an increase in illness at work from our mounting passion for computer use: headaches, stress, debilitating illnesses that come from a weakened personal energy field.

To absorb negative energy from computers

A simple way to help alleviate the effects of the negative energy emitted from computers is to place a pyrite by each one.

If it is a work environment, or you work a lot at home using a computer, then know that your pyrite, if placed beside each machine, will work very hard indeed. It would be advisable to have two sets of pyrite for such use and to alternate them at the end of each week, allowing the redundant set to "rest" in a vessel of water for at least 24 hours. Once cleansed and ready to work again, these pyrite clusters or cubes should be held in the right palm and asked *to absorb all negative magnetic energy emitted from the computer and to render your environment pure and clear and harmonious.*

Remember, like a television, what your computer shows is then magnified into your home, unless you use a pyrite. Always avoid negative use of the computer; you actually draw this energy within your home or workplace, so even if you hold no respect for your own energy field—and I am sure you do—please respect the energy fields of others: your family, or colleagues perhaps. Pyrite will help you improve the environment for them.

I have a friend who works in promotional production. She and her colleagues were complaining of feeling exhausted with all the equipment in their editing suite. She took some pyrite to try it out and placed a piece beside each machine. Undaunted by her colleagues' comments about "funny little rocks" sprouting up everywhere, she was delighted to be inundated by their acknowledgments that they did feel better—more energized, less tired, less prone to eye strain and headaches.

Cell phones

Some would say that these communication tools are the plague of the planet. I like talking more than most; however, the intrusion and sheer energy spend of seeking and talking so much is a severe drain on our energy fields. Cell phones do emit a highly negative charge and I, personally, firmly believe that somewhere on our planet scientists know that and have proven that fact, yet I feel that it will be like the case of smoking; whether or not that research gets published publicly or not depends on who has paid for it, therefore the rest of us will only officially find out when great swathes of people have fallen ill in the wake of that highly negative emission from something like a cell phone.

If you do need to use a cell phone (and most of us do), then use one responsibly and in acknowledgment of your energy field.

Note the illustration of what the energy from a cell phone looks like when on and off. Pretty scary, isn't it? Please also note the same cell phone after it has been placed beside a piece of pyrite for an hour—a very positive difference, I am sure you will agree.

Cell phone "on"

Cell phone "off"

Cell phone placed beside pyrite for one hour

The second illustration shows the cell phone "off," that is to say it is switched on but not active. Therefore, here the energy coming from the cell phone is green, denoting the battery is on but there is not a charge going through it.

The next illustration shows the cell phone "on" and actively receiving a call. There are vivid red flashes of negative energy, which, if you pick this phone up, will run up your arm or attach to your ear.

The illustration of the cell phone after being placed beside a pyrite for an hour shows the charge of negative energy has reduced, being absorbed by the pyrite.

Perhaps one day cell phone companies will supply free pyrite with simple instructions for its use every time they sell a cell phone, allowing people the ability to protect themselves and take responsibility, just as they should, for selling a product that is so energy- and health-challenging.

Please be particularly careful with children and cell phones. Children have sensitive, developing energy (not to mention developing brains), yet they are very eager to be cell phone users. Please take care. I believe no one under the age of 12 should have prolonged use of a cell phone in order to be protected from their overuse, and up to age 16 access to mobile devices should be limited.

To energy cleanse a cell phone

Place the cell phone, together with its charger, beside a piece of pyrite overnight. Prior to setting this up, cleanse the pyrite, then hold it in your right palm and ask that *the pyrite absorb all the negative electromagnetic emissions and transmute them, then veil the phone and you with the energy of peace and protection.*

You can carry pyrite in a pouch, pinned to your person, if you are an avid cell phone user; in which case, cleanse the pyrite each day in water for a minimum of four hours, or overnight.

Leave a programmed piece of pyrite in your car (cleanse it regularly, at least weekly), asking that it *absorb all electromagnetic emissions from your phone and the electrical system of your car, and veil you and your car with the energy of peace, clarity, and focus so that you may be attentive and safe as you drive.*

Pyrite for personal use

Pyrite is a useful healing tool for you also. If you have a "stubborn" energy in any area of your life (everyone has this, usually a deeply ingrained pattern born of many past lives of experience, where we have become quite literally stuck in the groove), you may carry a piece of pyrite in a pouch, which you can cleanse and ask *to help absorb that negative energy, which creates imbalance within you, that you may be of greater ease, flow, and peace in your life.* Try it—it is a powerful healing tool.

Programming pyrite

See page 42 for more information on how to program crystals.

For personal use

I ask the Light [or earth energies] to please charge this crystal to veil [full name or our home] with healing for [healing focus]. Thank you.

For professional use

I call upon the Light, please charge this crystal with the highest positivity to veil [full name] with the Light of/for [healing focus]. I thank the Light.

Examples of healing focus:
- Absorb negative electromagnetic energy (general appliances)
- Absorb negative electromagnetic energy (specific appliances, e.g., microwave)
- Absorb negative electromagnetic energy from television/transmitted negative program
- Absorb negative electromagnetic energy from computer/laptop and so on
- Absorb negative electromagnetic energy from cell phone
- Personal release of stubborn negative patterning

Celestite

Healing qualities:

Celestite crystal can draw the angelic consciousness of spiritual rays to you:

The ray of healing

The ray of wisdom

The ray of protection

The ray of love

The ray of service

The ray of strength

The ray of divine consciousness (spiritual attunement)

Celestite has such a gentle, encouraging energy that children are naturally drawn to its radiance. It is the crystal of focus to use when assisting or working with the chronically ill or dying. We could all do with divine help and the loving support of angelic consciousness. Working with celestite we have the gift of bringing forth the many angelic rays to work with us in our everyday lives.

This is the "angelic crystal." This gracious crystal connects us to angelic consciousness. The name celestite comes from "celestial of Light." We could all do with a greater, stronger, and more frequent connection to angelic consciousness and in particular, to our own assigned angels, who are always near, waiting patiently to be called, connected with, or spoken to. If you do nothing else spiritual today, say a bright "Hello!" to your angels and ask that your guardian angel, who knows you better than any other, better than you know yourself, can help you in some way that is very particular to you.

Your angels have traveled the ages with you, supported and nurtured you when you have made the "call"—where allowed by your divine plan. Perhaps your angel has even shown you a sign of their presence, a sign that they are really there with you.

With regard to signs, it is positive to be open to them in your life and ask for them often. The synchronicity of life is a joyous, miraculous, wondrous gift to us all, yet all too often we give way in our minds and put a significant sign down to coincidence, not accepting that we are perhaps worthy of the many miracles of connection with which we are blessed every single day. We should, rather, acknowledge that we are blessed and open our hearts to the universe, which is constantly seeking to converse with us, all around us, in a multitude of different ways. Speak back to the universe, call on your angels often, then the whole miraculous process of synchronicity increases. I urge you to open up to communing with your angels.

Celestite can help you to connect to angelic consciousness, as well as assisting you and those around you in many other ways.

Angels operate at the request of the divine and mankind as an interface of consciousness to help us with our earthly plight. Angels cannot intervene if it is not in our life plan for them to do so, yet so often we do not make use of their gift of blessings of Light and energy for the simple reason that we fail to call them. Angels cannot step in unless they are asked.

Prayer is a natural way to communicate to your angels your particular needs; for example, meditating on an "angelic focus"—say a picture of Lord Michael, archangel of the blue ray of spiritual strength and protection—and calling upon his Light to veil you is a very protective energetic gift to employ. Remember, if prayer is asking, meditating is listening.

If you wish to use crystals to enhance your call to the Light and to help your energy to open up to angelic consciousness, simply take a small lump of celestite that has been cleansed and hold it in your right palm. Ask the celestite *to connect you to the angels of the blue ray to protect you and to veil you in their spiritual strength.* Thank your angels, then place your celestite in a pouch or in your pocket.

You can also wear a cleansed celestite pendant over your heart chakra. If you require connection to the angels of healing, vary the words you use in your call accordingly. For example: *I call upon the angels of healing to veil me with the Light of healing, through this celestite, to help me to be of greater patience. I thank the Light and the angels of healing.*

You can ask your celestite to connect you to all angelic consciousness, if you so wish. However, you may find you have a greater clarity of awareness if you choose no more than three streams of angelic consciousness to connect to at any one time. For example: Hold the cleansed celestite in your right palm and ask the crystal *to connect you to the angels of the rays of love, wisdom, and divine consciousness for that day.* Thank the angels, then place the celestite in a pocket or pouch.

You can use celestite to facilitate connection to the divine through sleep. Before going to sleep at night, hold the cleansed celestite in your right palm and ask *that the crystal facilitate your connection to Light and your healing, teaching, and spiritual development. Thank your crystal and then place it under your pillow while you sleep.* It is possible to connect to teachings for your life plan through dreams and I know some people who connect to masters of the Light, in their spiritual ashrams of Light around the planet, during their sleep. Remember, on waking, to cleanse your crystal, then align yourself and protect your energy field before beginning the day.

Celestite, for me, is the most useful crystal to help in connection with my children. You cannot be with your children all the time and nor should you be ultimately. I align my children, as I have discussed earlier in the book, together with using techniques to protect their energy. Yet I cannot describe the relief of asking that angels of the Light walk with them, be with them, and protect them throughout each and every day. It is something I pray for each day. Teach your children about angels; children naturally gravitate to the idea of angels, usually love the concept of angels, and feel reassured that they have this "Light protector" with them, on call.

I place celestite in a pouch, then pin the pouch to my children's clothing (along with other personal healing crystals) and I find the children just get on with the day and the pouch means you don't keep losing the crystals. Well, in theory—when my eldest son was small he often gave crystals away to more needy individuals in the playground at school, which they gratefully received.

The method I use: I ask that the cleansed celestite *draws angelic consciousness to my children, to protect them and keep them safe and well, held in the Light of the angels of love, wisdom, and protection—seated in the blue ray of Archangel Michael.* I thank the crystals and the angels, then place the celestite in the pouch, pin the pouch to a trouser pocket, and off they go. Believe me, it is a great relief to know that angels walk with you and that you can call upon their divine love and help for others around you also.

Celestite can be called upon to veil the Light of healing to a sick or dying person. It is important to clarify here that "healing" does not always mean that you survive illness if your life plan dictates otherwise; however, healing in the true sense can occur up to and beyond death. That is because healing, in truth, is the betterment of dis-ease in our body/energy field; dis-ease always occurs first in the energy field and then tracks through the physical body. Our physical body may disintegrate through dis-ease; we transmute our negativity in that way and what we do not transmute we carry in our energy "coats" back to the Light. On our return to a physical incarnation here, we have to collect the energy coat and bring it back again in order to release that negativity. The more you release in the life, the better. If you acknowledge illness as a teacher and that dis-ease can be released up to and beyond death, then use celestite to draw the angels of healing to a sick or dying person in order that they receive help to bear their plight and their soul learning as their soul wishes —they may require 'patience' or 'fortitude' or 'spiritual strength' in the face of great challenge and adversity. All these experiences are very difficult and exactly when you would want troops and legions of angels all around you, to hold you in Light and divine consciousness.

For my friend who was tragically dying of cancer, we programmed a celestite and placed it in her room. It was a large, beautiful, sparkly piece of crystal and a joy both to look at and to touch. We asked that it be charged with Light to be a beacon of Light for the angels to connect to my friend, that she would be spiritually strengthened toward her journey home to the Light in peace, joy, and in harmony with all beings around her. It was a beautiful and moving process to be involved in and very healing to all of us to help a dear person that we loved so much with her challenging plight. I can only say that it is an empowering thing to do for a relative or friend of someone in the same position as my friend. What could be better than to promote Light, for the person passing from their life, through prayer and the use of crystals. It is a joyous gift to give.

It is always better to pray for a sick or a dying person with a focus on prayer for their strength to make their choices according to their soul's wish. It is important to respect the divine will and the choices of another soul (do not pray for someone to live) and not to impact our will or wish on another at a time when they may require all our help and Light to focus on them, to help make that final journey home to Light for themselves, for it is their soul's wish to do so. That person's individual soul plan should be held within highest regard and focus.

Celestite to draw angelic consciousness to your home

Celestite is simply lovely to use in your home as a device to draw angelic consciousness into greater abundance and increased awareness for you there.

Place a piece in the heart of your home—the kitchen, always the heart of any home. Cleanse the celestite and ask that it be charged to veil your home with the Light to connect to the angels of peace, love, and protection. Your home will feel wonderful.

Celestite to protect a person traveling

If someone you love is traveling, you could ask a celestite crystal to travel with them and thus take with them the veil of Light of your love and angelic consciousness to protect and hold them safe.

Cleanse the celestite and hold the crystal in the right palm and ask accordingly: *I ask that this celestite crystal be charged with Light protection to travel with [say the name of the person who requires the crystal]. Thank you.*

Celestite to create a sanctuary space

A special and lovely way to use celestite is to create a sanctuary space in your home for prayer and meditation. Keep the space simple, perhaps a candle or fresh flowers—a rose has a very high, pure energy vibration to meditate with. You could include a cleansed piece of celestite, which may be asked *to veil the sanctuary space with a connection to angels working on the ray of divine consciousness as well as strengthening your connection to your own team of angels—that you may have greater connection and awareness to them throughout your everyday life.*

Place your celestite next to a candle and meditate for 10–20 minutes.

Programming celestite

See page 42 for more information on how to program crystals.

For personal use

I ask the Light [or earth energies] to please charge this crystal to veil [full name] with healing for/to [healing focus]. Thank you.

For professional use

I call upon the Light, please charge this crystal with the highest positivity to veil [full name] with the Light of/for [healing]. I thank the Light.

Examples of healing focus:
- Facilitate connection to angelic consciousness, such as the angels of healing, of wisdom, of protection, of unconditional love, of strength, of service, of divine consciousness
- Angelic protection for a child
- Angelic protection for travel
- Angelic connection for the sick or dying
- Draw angelic presence to your home
- A sanctuary space connected to the energy of peace and divine consciousness
- Angelic connection to Light healing, or Light wisdom, or Light guidance (during sleep)
- Angelic assistance for the end of life

Smoky Quartz

Healing qualities:

Powerful absorber of negativity

Powerful transmuter of karma (sacred cosmic laws)

The healing stone for "assumption" (assumption = belief systems, control issues, arrogance, tendency to presume)

This crystal is a powerful healer's tool used in crystal circuitry and on that basis, one of the crystals I use several times, most days, in my therapy practice. It is the crystal that can help you, on a personal level, realise the fullest potentials of your lifeplan, or help you free yourself if you have "control" issues. It is also one half of the amazing car karma crystals, which can help to absorb the negative energy from the cars we drive and help us balance our karma with the earth.

The smoky quartz orb

This beautiful, powerful crystal has a very special capacity in an orb shape. Orbs are a whole area of crystal work on their own, therefore part of very advanced practice as they require greater care, attention, and respect.

Orbs can be so powerful as to make you feel unwell if not used properly and appropriately, depending on which orb you work with. I say this only as a precaution, as orbs can be high attainment crystal power tools that may fulfil interests in astral travel, or desires to connect to guides and masters in the Light. Some people might use orbs in a way that they are not prepared for energetically. Better to build up to working with the more powerful crystals and enjoy the journey. There is nothing wrong with desiring high attainment; it is to be admired and rewarded, when you are ready. Be sure that the Light will reward you with gifts aplenty when you are ready—that is, when the Light deems you are ready. If you are not ready, the Light will also challenge your ego and self-attainment. Who and what are you seeking, why, and to what end? That is because all your life experience is to show you and teach you about yourself.

Having said all this, please be very assured that the smoky quartz orb is safe to use. I outline here some of the optimum ways you can work with it.

Greater connection to the soul plan

One way to use the smoky quartz orb is to first cleanse it by placing it in water then, holding it in your right palm (or if it is too large, place the crystal on a table and place your right palm over it), simply ask *that the smoky quartz crystal orb be charged with Light to help you and your family, and all who come into your home, to transmute all negative karmic connections and to receive spiritual support toward understanding your soul journey together.*

Then place the orb in a central place in the home where everyone will pass by it, therefore passing through the energy emissions of the smoky quartz. What will happen is that each time a person passes through this radiating Light, he or she will have an energy cleansing of their four lower bodies, together with an infusion of Light that will help each person in greater connection to their spiritual plan, that which they wrote in the Light before their present incarnation on Earth.

For example, you may have had a yearning to visit Peru when younger. Over time you have forgotten that pull to go there, yet in your soul plan this has an importance for you and you have asked to be reminded of it because Peru offers you great opportunities for your spiritual strengthening and for greater connection to soul friends.

If you visit Peru, for example, even on holiday, you will walk roads and paths that you have walked before in other lives of great strength and ability, when you were accomplished in all matters concerning energy. When you walk through the energy of the smoky quartz orb you will receive a cleansing of energy and you will also get a "tap, tap, tapping" from your soul, now awakened in your energy field, that means all of a sudden you start to see Peru everywhere, such as in papers and on TV. This is the universe conspiring to nudge you toward your divine plan and point you at Peru. Such is the beauty of the synchronicity of life and such is the beauty of the smoky quartz orb, which can ignite within you direction, from your soul, toward advancing your life plan and all your positive potentials.

Such an orb does not need to be large in size. In crystal shops, geological quality often makes orbs very expensive, but there is no need to select one according to this. I have seen and experienced orbs that are very cloudy, with no real physical purity in their appearance (they have inclusions and marks), and yet when you begin to work with these orbs, amazingly, they clear. Likewise, I have seen orbs with great beauty and clarity purchased at great cost that develop "clouds," marks, and inclusions that were not there previously. The flaws are showing you something. They are reflecting back to you the impurity, fog, or manifestation in your life that you require to transmute. If you have an orb of another crystal persuasion, for example, a rose quartz or snow quartz, and you have seen this happen, meditate with your orb and ask to be shown what within your life you need to clear—to transmute and heal.

The rutilated smoky quartz orb

Another special orb to use at home in the smoky quartz family is the rutilated smoky quartz orb. These are very powerful crystals that help with releasing and understanding your karmic connections, that which you have to achieve for the life; that which you have to "walk" through and master in order to step up on your soul journey. Each rutile thread within the orb represents a karmic connection to clear.

I obtained just such an orb some years ago and was guided to meditate with it whenever I felt resistance or difficulty in my life. At the time it came to me, life felt like a constant struggle and I noticed that the rutiles within seemed to grow denser and denser. After meditating on people, places, and events that were occurring in my life, I gained greater insights into the learning for the life that my soul was showing me. I was being pushed hard to let go of old patterns and ways that I had carried for many lives but did not suit or work for me now. This meditational tool of instruction was very helpful to me. I urge everyone to have a go at meditating with a rutile smoky quartz orb to open yourself to cosmic insights. Be prepared to confront and release your own rubbish in order that you may walk forward to greater empowerment and joy in your life.

Meditating with a rutilated smoky quartz orb

For such a meditation, place the orb before you on a table, then sit in a straight-backed chair (having previously cleansed the orb by placing your hands over it and asking the Light *that all negativity be released from its being and the highest peace and Light be charged to its being for your personal meditation*). Close your eyes and feel the peace. Allow 10–15 minutes to meditate. Cleanse the orb upon completion of the meditation, then put it away, wrapped carefully to avoid any damage.

Smoky quartz eggs

Using these crystal eggs forms a working acknowledgment of your karma on Earth, in taking personal responsibility and processing that karma. By that, I mean each day we are here we are all using the energy of the Earth. We either use it positively, giving gratitude and joy to the Earth in return for her bounty and replenishing Earth's energy as we are able to do, or we are taking from the Earth in greed, selfishness, perhaps also "dumping" on the Earth in a careless and negative way. I know it sounds awful to put it so starkly; however, it is true that while none of us want to think or feel that we are using the Earth's resources or energy so negatively that we are hurting our planet, very sadly, on a daily basis, we are doing precisely that.

Earlier in this book we discussed negative magnetic energy emissions in the home (see the section on pyrite, page 72) and in that section I described to you what that negative energy emission looks like in your home. Unchecked by pyrite, that negative magnetic energy emission from all your appliances magnifies out all over your street, town, county, country, and so on around the planet. From a planetary perspective, this negative energy magnetizes to polar sites—particularly polar north. Next time they show global warming on the television and the breakdown of the ozone layer around our beautiful planet Earth, look hard at where that focus is: polar north. We are microwaving our ice cap with our unchecked use of our household appliances, our chemicals, our company and industrial waste.

We will all reap our karma for this creation, which is a wholly man-made devastation, and we are collectively reaping it now. Do not be downcast or depressed about this fact; instead, be positive and responsible. You can do something about it and you can start doing it right now. You can make a significant positive change and effect great transmutation in this matter, and one huge way to begin is to start to use pyrite in your home (as described in the pyrite section, see page 72) and to use smoky quartz eggs.

Absorbing negative energy emissions from your car

Every time you and I get in our cars and drive we are creating negative karma for ourselves, unless we are actively doing something to direct our creation of negative energy (and damage to the planet) into the Earth in order that the Earth may transmute that negative energy. By doing this we are taking responsibility for that which we create during our time on the planet. It is a good way to take responsibility for our mode of transport. A car throws out a lot of "rubbish" in energy terms, and we all leave a trail of this negative energy everywhere we drive, with our name on it. By the laws of karma, we all have to rebalance this energy. We can elect to do it now by taking personal responsibility; if we do not, we must take our soul consequences, which will mete out that rebalance for us and these may not be so palatable to us when they come our way.

It is useful to have **two** sets of the following crystals in order that you may wash/cleanse them overnight each week, then rest the cleansed set for the remainder of the week, using the alternate set in your car. Then do the same and rotate the sets of crystals in your car the following week. It is important that these crystals go into water overnight to cleanse them as they will be working very hard on your behalf.

Take two smoky quartz eggs, sometimes referred to as dragon's eggs. These are rounded and have the capacity to absorb much negative energy. Do not choose a smoky quartz with any kind of point or directional feature for this particular use.

You will also require a rounded chunk of rose quartz—again, two pieces. The rose quartz and the smoky quartz should both be no smaller than an inch and a half (4cm) in diameter.

Wash one set of these car karma crystals (a rose quartz and a smoky quartz) separately, then hold the rose quartz in your right palm and ask *that the rose quartz veil your car with peace, that you may flow in peace and harmony and positivity wherever you travel.* Place the rose quartz in the front of the car, centrally if possible. I do not smoke, so I find that the ashtray is a suitably accommodating space to place this crystal. If the crystal does not fit, use the glove compartment, as long as this is a space that is free from clutter; crystals do not like clutter as it is a manifestation of confused energy, so keep these spaces where you place crystals clean and clear. Remember, crystals absorb and magnify energy and we wish to magnify clarity, positivity, and peace—not clutter.

Next, take the smoky quartz crystal, hold that in your right palm, and ask that the smoky egg *absorbs all negative energy emissions from your car, that you may release positively and responsibly all your karmic residue wherever you go, that it may be released to the Earth for transmutation at this time with the aid of the crystal.* Thank the Light, thank the Earth, thank the crystal.

Then place the smoky quartz egg into your boot/trunk space, again centrally if you are able. Place the crystal in a protective pouch to protect it from knocks and bangs or chips; chips in the crystal will affect the flow of energy emission and absorption, so if one of these crystals breaks, please get another. In my car, I have secured my smoky quartz in the space near the spare tire, then the mat for the boot lining goes over the top. I have known people tape their crystals in place. Remember, crystals like order and to be in free-flowing energy spaces.

When you place these crystals in water at the end of the week, you may notice that there is a discharge into the water (particularly from the smoky egg) that looks like a petrol puddle, that cloudy rainbow effect that puddles sometimes have in parking lots. These crystals will be working very hard for you, so please look after them.

There is another benefit from using these crystals in this way, aside from the joy of being responsible with regards to your karma; that benefit is that you will be up to 25 percent more efficient in your fuel consumption. I have experienced this and I would urge you to be energy responsible and to give these crystals a try.

Using smoky quartz to heal yourself

Take a small, rounded smoky quartz and use it to help yourself release ingrained patterns of old ways. Ways that you have had for many lives, that no longer serve you any purpose, that now only curtail your true potential; sometimes these are the hardest patterns to shake off. Let me give you an example.

Some years ago, I had a client who was very gifted and enthusiastic about healing. She was a highly trained and qualified therapist yet she had somehow found herself surprisingly unable to keep her therapist practice going. She was concerned about her own healing program and what it was that the universe was conspiring to show her, but needing funds she resorted to working part-time as a secretary—her previous job. She was active in her life learning and had regular therapy herself; however, she had failed (despite having tremendous understanding, insights, and intuition) to action "new" energy into her life as an antidote to her issues (all acknowledged and accepted by her) of control.

The more control you apply in life, the more life conspires to show you that you have no control. The antidote here is to let go; ask, ask,

ask, the universe to facilitate your learning and most importantly your ability to change, really change. You have to change and if you do not, then by cosmic law, you will attract the same lessons back, time and again, and this can happen over many lives. It may be different people, different places, different times but the lesson is the same and until it is mastered, that same lesson will prevail. The trick is to identify the lesson, learn it and learn it quickly, and then move on.

To help my client with her difficulty, we did much "soul recall" work (past-life therapy), life plan work, together with crystal healing, which included the personal homework of carrying a piece of smoky quartz (cleansed regularly), programmed for her use to help her release the energy of assumption. "Assumption" is a great word and it really sums it all up. Assumption = belief system, control patterns/issues, arrogance, and a tendency to presume.

If you feel you suffer from any of the above, and many of us do, then try this crystal work for yourself. It is very, very powerful and you will come to acknowledge and identify your responses and reactions to challenges in your life with new insight.

While holding a smoky quartz in your right palm, ask that the crystal *be charged with the highest positivity to cleanse you of all negativity pertaining to assumption and control issues, bringing you into peace, flow, and balance of your energy field*. Thank the Light.

Then, simply carry the crystal in a pouch in your pocket or pinned to your clothing daily. Cleanse each week in water.

Programming smoky quartz

See page 42 for more information on how to program crystals.

For personal use

I ask the Light [or earth energies] to please charge this crystal to veil [full name] with healing for [healing focus]. Thank you.

For professional use

I call upon the Light, please charge this crystal with the highest positivity to veil [full name] with the Light of/for [healing focus]. I thank the Light.

Examples of healing focus:

- The transmutation of karma
- Promoting higher insight through meditation to aid soul teaching/karmic release
- Absorbing negative emissions from the car ("car set": use together with rose quartz)
- Releasing the energy of "assumption" (control patterns)

Citrine

Healing qualities:

Physical cleanser

Emotional purifier

Promotes clean, clear energy (which vibrates in vitality and joy)

This is an amazing crystal to use for cleansing. It is a natural healer to the solar plexus chakra (emotional energy center). Citrine also supports the physical cleansing of your home and your environment.

For citrine—think lemon. I am convinced there are a thousand and one household uses for a lemon and nor is it any accident that household cleansers always have "lemon" attached to their ingredients because of its astringent, cleansing, and naturally antiseptic qualities.

Citrine may be placed in the dishwasher and/or dishwashing water to energy cleanse your dishes. Of course, you must physically cleanse your plates, utensils, and so on; however, if you could see the energy vibration attached to your dishwashing you would see that they are not always energy purified. What you need to do if you wish to energy cleanse your dishes is ask a citrine crystal *to absorb all negative energy from the pots and dishes that are placed in the machine/water*, then place the crystal in the sink or the dishwasher. (For this purpose, I place my citrine in the cutlery holder, where it firmly sits, working hard.)

Once the washing cycle/dishwashing is complete, place the citrine in a bowl of clean water for three hours (usually until the next time it is required). You could have a few citrines rotating for this purpose. They do look attractive in large jam jars in the kitchen, ready and waiting for use.

The same goes for floor and surface cleansing. There are really good chopping boards for food preparation and of course you must have high standards when it comes to physically cleansing food preparation areas and maintaining good physical housekeeping, but I would say add good energetic housekeeping to this also. However much you bleach a surface, you will never be able to bleach away negative energy.

I am no longer a meat eater, for example, but I eat fish occasionally. I went to an energy seminar many years ago where the speaker gave a demonstration about the energy attached to a slice of bacon. The speaker was a gifted energy sensor who could "see" the energy about him and "read" it accordingly. He was able to tell from that single slice of bacon that the particular pig that the bacon had come from had died in great trauma. The energy of that trauma was attached to the meat. We were all asked if we would want to eat that traumatized energy. He was also able to detect that the pig had not been well treated and held great fear; all that energy is contained in the meat, so to consume the meat is to consume that fear, trauma, and pain, not to mention all the other issues that surround how our farm animals are fed, and which pass into the food chain (for example, vegetarian animals fed dried carcasses of other animals).

We need food to replenish our physical energy. Surely our bodies deserve the purest energy, or we shall suffer the consequences. People do not consider the energy effects of food on their physical bodies, never mind their emotional, mental, or spiritual bodies.

It is possible to energy cleanse your food. You can call in prayer with the food in front of you and ask the Light *that the food be cleansed of all negative energy and that the negative energy be released to the Earth for transmutation of this time.* Then ask in prayer *that your food be invested with Light, positive energy, and peace to fulfil and sustain your health and well-being.*

Once you have asked a cleansed piece of citrine to energy purify the food that you prepare, place the crystal on your work surface in a central position, where it will draw negative energy off the food. It is really useful to place a few pieces of cleansed citrine into your fruit bowl and your breadbox. Your fruit and bread will remain fresher longer and will be more energy-positive for your consumption.

Let's move away from the kitchen to the bathroom and think about toilets. Toilets are where we release our physical waste, so it is very useful to place a dedicated citrine nearby. (Never use a kitchen citrine for this. Always have a set of kitchen citrines and a bathroom set.) Those of you who are energy aware will understand about the metaphysical meaning of dis-ease, and you will know that if you are constipated you have a lack of flow to your emotional energy, now not flowing physically; you are not letting go of your rubbish, literally. If you suffer from diarrhea, you have emotional overflow, therefore you are in emotional flux and turmoil. If you suffer from either of these complaints, a holistic reflexologist will help you bring balance to your body and energy field through finding the root cause of your complaint and you could carry a programmed fluorite to help to "flow you right."

It is useful practice to raise the positive energy around the toilet in the home. Toilets work away, using water to process our waste and carry it off out of sight—but where does it go? Again, mostly we do not care as long as we do not have to deal with it. To energy cleanse that which you release and to cleanse yourself upon releasing it (whatever it is), together with the area of release (the toilet and surrounding space), program a large chunk of citrine and place it on the floor at the back of the toilet area.

Ask that the citrine *be charged to absorb all negative energy from this space and the functions within this space, that the negative energy be absorbed by the crystal and transmuted at this time, and that the space be replenished with the energy of peace, harmony, and flow.*

A cleansing drink (citrine)

Crystals and gems can charge pure spring water very effectively to provide all manner of healing to your body and your energy field.

The way "gem remedies" work is very similar to a tuning fork. All crystal healing is about "molecular resonance." If I strike a tuning fork, it makes a note that can be followed. If I use a crystal on your chakra, the chakra will awaken and "remember" its true, perfect, positive state of being, its optimum state of being. The chakra yearns to follow the note, the vibration of its true, positive beauty. Many methods of healing work in this way: an awakening of the energy field, a reminder of the purity the chakra can achieve, a release of the sluggish, held negativity. The crystal is the vehicle that charges the energy field in order that it may flow in great beauty and positivity.

True healing reflects a total change throughout all the bodies of the human energy field. You can, through crystal healing, ignite great flow in your energy field, release your rubbish (which has accumulated over many years), and be charged and aligned in Light energy so that you have a virtually new body. Your energy matrix and the life plan that is encoded to your cellular structure can be restructured and in turn there is the possibility, with the "will of the soul," that dis-eases can be transmuted in a way that was previously not thought possible. If your life plan dictates and facilitates such an opportunity, much can be achieved. If it does not, much can be achieved in another way.

A cleansing gem remedy to make at home

Fill a pitcher or tumbler with fresh, pure spring water (do not use tap water, as it has a low vibration). You can charge this directly, with the crystals placed in the pitcher itself. Alternatively, place the pitcher of water in a large glass bowl and pour more spring water into the bowl to a depth of about 2 inches (5cm). Place four citrines (round, tumbled pieces will suffice) in a cross shape around the pitcher, inside the bowl. The citrines must be cleansed beforehand. To do this, hold them in your right palm and ask *that they be cleansed of all negative energy and that the negative energy be released to the earth for transmutation.* Then to program the citrines, place them again in your right palm and ask *that they purify the water and charge it with the Light of energy cleansing to the physical, emotional, and mental bodies of this time.* Place the citrines in the bowl and leave to charge for three hours.

After three hours, remove the citrines, place a seal over the water in the pitcher (to keep it clean and dust-free), and keep the pitcher refrigerated. Consume over three days to enhance the cleansing and releasing of toxicity in the body. Eat lightly (for example, fresh salads) and after three days you will feel a sense of inner cleanliness.

Reserve the water that surrounded the pitcher in the bowl (the water that contained the citrines themselves), as you can use this to water your plants and to revitalize the soil in your garden.

A note about the citrine cleansing remedy: do not be surprised if you have frequent or loose bowel motions, although you may not have anything like that at all. If you experience this kind of release, all will rebalance upon completion of your energy cleansing. See it as a positive release of energetic holding from your body and your energy field.

To facilitate a revitalizing and joyous energy

Who would not wish to have such a disposition in life, yet we are often laid low by life and find ourselves feeling lacking in energy or any kind of joyous spirit. The zest for life that we had as children, where we found the world full of wonder and delight, has sadly been buried by worry and anxiety and sometimes it is challenging to get it back.

To revive a joyous, energized feeling, place a large citrine in a central point within your home or workplace. Make sure you have cleansed it first and then program it by placing your right palm over it and asking *that the citrine charge the energy around it with great purification, vitality, and joyousness.* Then leave the crystal to work for you to facilitate these qualities. Cleanse the citrine each week in water, pat it dry, and then ask it to do the same again for you, simply repositioning the citrine to set it to work.

You can place citrine on a stone cairn for use outside and for the same purpose; however, I would urge you to choose carefully and appropriately where you place such a cairn. Someone once asked me about a cairn like this one for a nursery garden for young children, but young children are usually joyous and boisterous enough, are they not? A crystal to encourage calm may be of greater purpose for a children's nursery, such as a rose quartz.

Programming citrine

See page 42 for more information on how to program crystals.

For personal use
I ask the Light [or earth energies] to please charge this crystal to veil [full name] with healing for/to [healing focus]. Thank you.

For professional use
I call upon the Light, please charge this crystal with the highest positivity to veil [full name] with the Light of/for [healing focus]. I thank the Light.

Examples of healing focus:
• Energy cleanse the dishwasher and its contents
• Energy purify and light charge food
• Energy purify bathrooms
• Facilitate vitality and joyousness

Fluorite

Healing qualities:

Enhances flow

Facilitates spiritual connection

Transmutes negativity

A key stone for releasing negative
karmic patterns

A strengthening stone for
life paths of difficulty

Fluorite is very beautiful and comes in many
amazing colors. For our purposes, we are
looking for a fluorite of a violet persuasion.
Do not worry if you have a "watermelon"
fluorite; as long as there is a predominance
of violet within the stone, you can put it to
work on the healing uses outlined below.

Fluorite = "flow you right." Remember this when you use fluorite. For example, if you feel you have sluggish energy, you can use fluorite by carrying it in a pocket or a pouch to promote greater positive energy flow about your total being.

Let's say that I have poor circulation in my lower legs. I am having regular reflexology, which will help me enormously, along with massage to stimulate my circulation and "soul recall" to get to the root cause of why I have this particular difficulty in the first place. While I am working hard doing all this to alleviate my difficulty, I also enlist the help of my fluorite. I cleanse the crystal and then I ask it *to be charged to help me to "flow" and for release of my holding and rubbish, that I may be of greater "flow" and release.*

The fluorite will enhance my transmutation of negativity; it will enhance my understanding of that negativity, and it will push my energy around and through my energy meridians and the energy circuitry through my chakra system to promote flow of my total being. With all of this work and my use of fluorite, I will see great improvement in my condition and I may possibly release the condition altogether.

My difficulty may be manifesting in another way that blocks the flow in my life. I may have a lack of flow to my funds. I may require funds for an important trip I wish to make. I have always wanted to go to Peru, but I lack the funds to fulfil my dreams. What shall I do?

Cleanse a fluorite and place it in a central place in your home. Place your right palm over the crystal and ask that the fluorite *facilitates great flow to your life and to your finances to attract to you the wherewithal to fulfil your life plan.*

Meditate on flow in your life. Ask yourself why the universe would not send you the means to have the funds if you are truly meant to be doing whatever it is that you wish to do/achieve. It may be that you have work to do first, or connections to release or to make in order to facilitate this event.

Please help the universe to help you. I have encountered people who feel that all they have to do is sit back and the connection will land in their laps. This happens, but it is rare. More usually, you are required by cosmic law to fulfil your share of effort to attain the gifts of connection. Look closely at your true efforts toward your alignment to your life path; look at what you wish of life from the heart and not your head. You may be surprised by what you intuit.

Using fluorite for spiritual connection

It is possible to use violet fluorite to help you to connect to your spiritual guides, to your spiritual masters, and to your "higher self." To do this, first cleanse two pieces of violet fluorite and ask *that the fluorite facilitate greater spiritual connection, through meditation, to your guides and masters in the Light.* Sit cross-legged on the floor (or on a cushion), straighten your back if you can, or use a straight-back chair and sit with your knees apart, feet flat to the floor, hands resting lightly on your thighs. Hold a violet fluorite in each palm for a few moments, then call to the Light: *Masters in the Light, please help me of this time…* Then begin your time of peace and meditation with the crystals. Keep to around 10–20 minutes and be assured that during this time you will, with practice, receive much insight, as there is a timelessness to meditation. Connection to Light exists beyond physical time. Do not feel tempted to spend a long time in meditation with a crystal; this can cause difficulties with alignment following long meditations. It is helpful to have a bath after a crystal meditation; a good long relaxing bath of even 30 minutes helps to realign your energy field and render you of greater clarity.

Releasing karma in the home positively

For this you need to enlist the help of a violet fluorite "octahedron." These crystals are beautiful as well as powerful and, like all crystals, need to be treated with considerable respect.

Karma, as we have discussed earlier in this book, is your "due" energy. It is the energy of balance. It may be that you have accrued these dues from other lives and from other people who are now with you again, and they are giving to you, energetically, in connection to releasing their karma. It may be that you have asked for karmic attainment yourself, for this life, and you have chosen a life of service to another, say a sick relative or friend. It may be that in your frustration with your lot in life, you are not seeing the karmic opportunities for your soul development and growth. Maybe you are faced with some hard choices and you are unable to choose, through either inertia or indecision, and need help to point the way.

A cleansed fluorite octahedron can be asked *to facilitate flow of karmic release, together with facilitating flow of karmic opportunity for all within the home in accordance with their soul's wish, that you have the strengthening and the Light to help you to achieve your optimum path of the soul.*

As you all pass through the emitting energy of the fluorite octahedron, you will each receive a "wash" of energy that cleanses your being, recharging and aligning you to the true wish of the soul. It is especially effective for the enhancement of flow between people.

The fluorite octahedron crystal and the difficult teenager

Let's say you have a difficult teenager in your midst. They are at a challenging age and you find yourself arguing and in disagreement with them most of the time. You could give the teenager a fluorite crystal pendant to wear or carry to quell this state of flux, but what can you do if they are uncooperative and will not wear one?

You could cleanse a fluorite octahedron, then place it in a central point in the home, somewhere where all those living there, including your challenging teenager, will pass by, having asked the fluorite octahedron *to cleanse all negative energy eruption between you all [name the names of those who live within the house—full names, as it is a call of vibration to help the crystal to do the work], and that the crystal brings you all the Light of peace, strength, and harmony for you to fulfil your karmic promises to each other in Light and positivity.*

Try this and you will be amazed. I have used this myself, many times, and I enjoy the reports back from friends and clients who have tried it too. No one enjoys disharmony in a relationship, whatever the relationship is; everyone needs to be positive, learn, and give where they can, for we are all on a journey of karmic release as well as spiritual attainment.

Using a fluorite octahedron to improve harmony at work

You can use this method very successfully in a difficult work situation. I know people who have been bullied mercilessly at work and have been downtrodden by their employers, disempowered in the miserable situations in which they find themselves each day.

Using a cleansed fluorite octahedron, hold it in your right palm and ask *that it absorb the negative energy around the office/building that you work in, that the negativity may be released to the earth for transmutation, and that the crystal negate the energy of "attack" or "bullying," that all may instead flow in harmony, peace, and unification to complete the karmic journey together.*

Strengthening yourself for a life path of difficulty

It is useful to remember, for very difficult situations in life, that all life is an illusion and physical lives are short. We have all asked prior to coming into the life to be placed into certain situations to outplay roles and challenges in order to overcome them. With "soul counseling," you get help to step above the emotional mire and look at the "reality" of the situation that you are in. It is very strengthening and empowering to do this, if you get the opportunity.

Take a rounded piece of fluorite and cleanse it in water. Pat it dry with a clean cotton cloth, then hold it in your right palm and ask the fluorite *to veil you [or another person—say the full name] with the Light and the strength to sustain you in your difficulty at this at this time. Ask that the pain may be absorbed by the crystal [this can be physical, emotional, mental, or spiritual pain] then transmuted and that Light may replenish you to rebalance your four lower bodies.* Thank the Light.

For example: fluorite can be very helpful for people who suffer chronic illness and extreme pain. We have had experience of this in my family over a number of years and have been greatly helped by our use of crystals. For pain and inflammation, we have applied a cleansed and programmed fluorite to areas of the spine literally oozing with the release of the hot energy of pain—a great negative energy flux—with slow, gentle circling of the crystal on the physical body, then moving the crystal higher through the other bands of the energy field. This can help to take the pain down a few notches by absorbing the negative energy, making it a little more manageable for the sufferer. (If the skin is sensitive or broken, you could simply rest the crystal on a clean towel over the injury for five minutes, then wash the crystal and put it away.)

After this kind of use, it is best to wash the fluorite by soaking it in water for three hours. If you are working with a very sick or ill person, it is useful to have another fluorite at the ready, which could be programmed and placed beneath their pillow. The fluorite thus continues to work to help the person suffering such challenges with their karmic release.

This is a personal testament to the advantages of coping with physical pain; however, not all pain is physical. Some of the greatest pain and hardship we carry in our patterning for life or in the events we encounter in life, that hurt us the most deeply, are from emotional pain.

Emotional pain can be devastating. A deep cavernous hole to climb out of, yet climb out of it we must. Crystals are immensely powerful and helpful in dealing with all aspects of emotion. Emotional pain, unchecked, leaks energy, literally draining "universal energy," our true life blood, from our bodies, thereby leaving us weak and vulnerable. We leak more and more energy, then deeper into the mire we sink. Emotional pain, unchecked, will therefore eventually create dis-ease in our bodies, leading to disease in our physical bodies.

If you have not done so already, I would urge you both to read about and take Bach Flower Remedies. These were created in the 1930s by Dr Edward Bach, who was an amazing individual—a doctor of great achievement and renown, who firmly believed people should be treated for the source/root cause of their illness to avoid the manifestation of illness altogether. He saw many ill people, taking the time to find out about them, and realized that in almost all cases their illness was rooted in their emotional dis-ease. He therefore set about discovering the natural antidotes to man's negative emotional conditions, with the intuitive help of the Light.

Bach Flower Remedies are inexpensive, powerful, and they really work. There are also no contra-indications to their use. Like crystals, they vibrationally alter your emotional energy field and help to bring your four lower bodies back into balance and harmony.

Your four lower bodies are amazing; they are constantly seeking to rebalance, to find optimum flow and health, therefore they will respond well to any help or boost to this end. Bach Flower Remedies work well in conjunction with crystals and with gem remedies also.

To heal emotional energy issues, you have to work very hard. You must accept the challenge and actively, constantly, persistently work at change; at repatterning your energy into the glowing, beautiful, wondrous being that you truly are. You have forgotten that you are Light and that is, in truth, your pain. You are Light. See and believe in yourself as Light once more.

It is said that on this planet we have only two emotions, both of which we have greatly distorted. Love and Fear. It is said that that is all there is to it. You are either in one state or the other. By love, I do not mean "in love"—that is an illusory and highly charged state to fulfil a divine purpose of connection. By love, I mean a state of unconditional love. Most of us spend entire lifetimes without experiencing unconditional love. In truth, most love demands and places conditions in its demonstration. We should ask for Light help to be open-hearted and embrace all in unconditional love, especially those who are most challenging to us, for they are the greatest of our soul friends, here to teach us well about our own weaknesses.

We should hug people more. What you learn from a hug is how wooden and "held back" people often are. A hug should be "heart to heart"—a "soul to soul" expression and exchange of energy. A hug is both changing and releasing. A hug can be incredible and lift the most downtrodden. Air-kissing is a strange ritual of our times. Rather, the embrace of a hug is to hold someone momentarily in an exchange of Light. When you go to hug someone, approach the hug giving Light and unconditional love. You will be joyous, as it is a joyous energy to give and receive.

To heal emotional pain, you will require the help of a "soul therapist." You will also need to commit to a personal healing program, to a sustained one. You will benefit from taking remedies, doing affirmations, and calling to the angels for help, as well as being active and vigilant in cleansing your body and your energy field. You will need to learn to love yourself—lots! You will need to look in the mirror each day and tell yourself: *I am love. I am beautiful. I am Light. I am a divine spark of creation and I have a divine plan to fulfil. I require help and support to fulfil it. Please send the angels of Light to be with me on this day and allow me the joy of connection to those in the physical who will help to strengthen me. I thank the Light.*

Most of us have a big problem with the concept of loving ourselves. We know our nasty side, the thoughts and feelings that we do not like. We are not really that negative energy. It is not the truth of us, so we can choose to be in it and live it and outplay that lower energy or we can choose to live in Light, in the energy of joy and positivity, sharing our Light with all we encounter for no other reason than to shine Light, for that is what we have come to do, selflessly and in unconditional love.

If we manage that holding of Light and giving of Light, we shall be as the beacon that attracts only Light to us, and therefore we shall grow in Light. It is infinite how connected to and full of Light we can become.

If we do not love ourselves, how can we be expected to love anyone else? How can anyone love us? If you do love yourself unconditionally, spiritually, then you are wholly attuned to your divine mission to "serve the soul" and you will not look for energy from another person to fill your gaps. You will have whole energy and be Light sustained. In that energy, you will be attractive to other whole energy people. You will be connected and will have the opportunities to fulfil soul plans together, or to fulfil a karmic path together toward divine achievement for the right, Light reasons, not because you want to have kids, a new kitchen, or a certain lifestyle. We make many selections and choices in life from only one perspective, the physical, and then we are surprised when issues arise in challenges of emotional or mental energy. Issues that are truly of the heart are not what physically motivated people perceive of the heart—desire. Unconditional love knows no desire, it knows only giving in purity from the heart.

To heal an emotional challenge to you or another

Take a piece of violet fluorite that has been cleansed. Hold it in your right palm and ask that the fluorite absorb all your emotional rubbish and your negative mental constraints. Ask *that the fluorite transmute your pain, that you may align to the opportunities of your divine plan, see and receive Light and positivity through the energy of the fluorite.* Thank the Light and the crystal. Cleanse this fluorite daily in water and ask again, as above, before placing the crystal into a pouch to carry.

This fluorite will then wash your body and energy in violet (transmutational) Light and you will start to feel a lightening of your emotional burdens.

Then the fluorite will charge your energy with greater positivity and flow to render you stronger and more open to the divine potentials that you have chosen in the Light, once you have overcome, surpassed, and mastered your emotional energy. The fluorite will pulse out to you a radiance to sustain within you a strength of heart connection and a calming influence of energy over the area of the solar plexus chakra.

You can also choose to wear a fluorite pendant over the heart chakra, programmed in the same way.

Programming fluorite

See page 42 for more information on how to program crystals.

For personal use

I ask the Light [or earth energies] please charge this crystal to veil [full name] with healing for [healing focus]. Thank you.

For professional use

I call upon the Light, please charge this crystal with the highest positivity to veil [full name] with the Light of/for [healing focus]. I thank the Light.

Examples of healing focus:

- Promotes flow in life
- Promotes flow of karmic release (family karma)
- Strengthens a life path of difficulty
- Promotes the healing of emotional challenge

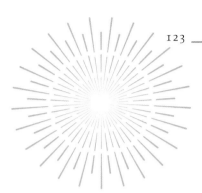

Unakite

Healing qualities:

Facilitator of universal Light to the environment

Promotes peace and balance

Unification

The crystal for community = "common unity"

This is the 'team' stone, the crystal that unites people towards a common goal; whether it's your sales team, or your football team, they will all perform better and more cohesively towards a defined aim with the aid of unakite. A wonderful tool for focussed meditation on bringing about the energy of peace, as well as for enhancing the positive energy of the environment. If you wish for more positive harmony in your world, begin to work with the wonder of unakite.

To make a cairn, take a group of rounded pebbles or stones that are suitable for forming its main shape, wash them down with water, and place them in a pointed mound shape in a free-flowing position in your garden (or terrace or patio). Free-flowing energy is one that will receive the freshness of the natural elements: fresh air, fresh water from the rain, and sunlight. All these natural elements will cleanse your cairn in perpetuity, once you have set up your stone mound and placed your cleansed, programmed crystal on the top.

Ask the unakite *to veil your place of living [or working] with the Light of peace and harmony to bring all together in unison of heart and flow, each to the other, radiating peace and balance of alignment to the focus of their common unity.*

"Common unity" is an interesting concept. We have all worked or perhaps lived in places where we feel everyone is pulling in very diverse directions, all with their own focus and self-need. This is a waste and dissipation of energy. In a working company situation, this scattered energy costs money; in a family or home environment, it can cost a great deal more, including energy-draining rows, friction, tension, unhappiness, or frustration.

When you are placed in a situation with other people (and you will be), either in your family or at work, you will be extremely lucky if you get on well with everyone, because the very nature of a life on Earth means you are here to balance karma. Perhaps you have a great "soul friend" from the Light, who has maybe, on this "soul incarnation," manifested as your mother-in-law. All of a sudden, in this life experience, all your irritations rise up as they reflect back to you that which you need to resolve.

In a challenging relationship, the issue is always not to change the behavior of another person, but to look at ways their behavior challenges you; you can only ever do something about you and you can never, ever, precipitate change in another, if they do not wish to change. You should see the challenge as an opportunity for your soul growth.

Perhaps, for example, your mother-in-law is domineering, irritating, and loud. Then she is showing you that you need to learn patience and greater inner peace, that you need to look at your own issues of control and your boundaries as well as your capacity for love—unconditional love.

If you use the experience positively, then you will grow as a soul and your attainment development can be great. If you feel negative in a situation, you should always use the opposite emotion to "rub out" the negativity. It has to be conscious and there will be ingrained patterns for you and the other person, so it will be tough and you will need to be vigilant and work hard.

Unakite will help facilitate the energy of harmony where there has been discord and it will strengthen your capacity to create the energy of peace and harmony where perhaps you have previously struggled.

Due to its amazing capacity to promote the energy of harmony, unakite is a great crystal to have as a large chunk in your home. It can be useful to place one in a hallway or kitchen as an ornamental, as well as functional, piece. You can ask that the unakite *veil your home and all within it in peace, balance, and harmony.* Cleanse the unakite weekly in water, reset the crystal in its place of working, and recharge it by asking again to ignite the unakite *to emit the powerful energy of peace, harmony, and balance throughout your home and to those who walk through its energy remit.*

Unakite is also a powerful healer in relationships where there has been dispute and disharmony. It can be washed in water and placed beneath the marital bed for those having difficulties in their relationship in order to realign to a common focus, where it is the life plan to effect this energy of harmony. In other words, if karmically you have completed your "job" together for this life and you are, from a soul perspective, destined to part, then the unakite will not unify you back to reigniting your relationship but will promote the energy of peace, harmony, and unification to your soul's wish and may help you facilitate a strong, aligned, and peaceful parting of the ways.

Unakite is the "team stone." If you like watching football and get a bit cross when you can see that your team are not aligned in play, perhaps performing like a bunch of strangers who have just met, imagine how your team could play if they were to make use of unakite. It is sad that with all the top-level sport psychology, coaching, and methods employed to help athletes in teams to focus on the end goal, few, if any, of these well-paid sports specialists have embraced the total healing, alignment, and strengthening of their four lower bodies. These sportsmen and women may be strong physically, but how strong are they with regard to their other energy bodies? Does the whole team have strength in their common focus?

Crystal work is as incredible in its use for teams in any sport as it is for individuals. Unakite, used for team meditations and programmed to be worn by players, has the capacity to align the combined energy of the individuals in the team and their efforts, in strength, toward the common goal.

Unakite is likewise great for sales teams, teaching teams, nursing teams, or for any job/project/goal where two or more people come together to perform a task.

To this end, it is very beneficial to have unakite in the boardroom of a company or in a common meeting place in order to unify flow in meetings and conferences where common focus is required.

Team meditation with unakite

Place a cleansed unakite centrally on a table or on the floor, with all the team members seated around it. Prior to the meeting, the cleansed unakite should be asked by one delegate (who places his/her right palm over the crystal) *to promote the energy of healing, peace, and common unity to all gathered around it.*

Take a few moments to sit together and breathe in the energy of the unakite, then begin your meeting. When the meeting is complete and everyone has left, remove the unakite and cleanse it in water, then put it away. When you want to use it again, cleanse the unakite and reprogram it by asking, as above.

It is possible to do group meditations with unakite—for example, for the energy of peace and harmony for planet Earth, or to direct the positive energy of peace and harmony to a specific site on the planet. Such group meditations work best with a minimum of 12 people seated around a unakite, placed centrally to the group. Sit in a circle, if possible, and place a lit candle (plain white) beside the unakite. A delegate should speak the words of focus for the group to introduce the meditation and should monitor the time (10–20 minutes only). The delegate should also close the meditation and bring everyone into alignment by a spoken method after no more than 20 minutes.

To program the unakite for a group meditation, before anyone enters the room the delegate should energy cleanse the crystal and arrange its position and that of the furniture. The energy of the room should be cleansed and the delegate should energy cleanse and align him/herself also. When fully prepared, the delegate should place the right hand over the unakite (which is in position) and ask the unakite *to facilitate the energy of peace and harmony to [at this point say the place name on the planet that your group wishes to send the Light of peace and harmony to—for example, Paris].* Then thank the Light.

Ask people to enter the room peacefully, quietly, even silently. Ask that they spend a few moments prior to entering the meditation space to align themselves in preparation to meditate and that they remain sitting quietly to await the introductory focus, which may be said like this, for example:

Close your eyes and breathe out. Be of peace and allow your mind to settle. Allow peace to fill and enfold your being. Let all tension release to the earth for transmutation of this time. Let peace fill your body and your energy field. Bring to your mind's eye the place of ["................."— whatever place is your choice of focus]. Allow your energy to focus on this place together with the Light of peace and harmony, that those who live in this place find peace in their hearts and a connection to greater harmony therein.

Then, after 20 minutes (in which the group silently maintain individual and collective focus to send Light to the place that you have chosen), the delegate may say, for example:

Breathe and allow your focus back to the unakite before you. Thank the crystal and your masters, guides, and angels from the Light, who have transmitted the Light of peace and harmony at this time. Know that the Light thanks you for your service to the Light. Be of peace.

And then for the alignment of those present at the meditation, the delegate may say, for example:

Breathe to the crown of the head. Draw to the crown the "Emerald Light of Alignment." Breathe down from the crown, drawing the emerald Light through the channel of the spine, down the legs, and into the feet. Breathe into the feet and feel your Light grounding to the earth of this time. Breathe across the body, draw the emerald Light through the shoulders, down the arms, and into the hands to the tips of the fingers and thumbs.

Be of balance and alignment, grounding your Light to the earth at this time, straight and strong, ready to open your eyes in your own time.

Notice that in the focus of the meditation we are specific about what Light we sent to this place. We asked for the "Light of peace and harmony." It is important to be specific. These meditations of focus are powerful and work hard on our behalf. Remember, we do not want to send Light to magnify the dark, therefore we must not send Light inappropriately. If you were sending Light—unfocused, unspecified—to all those in, say, a war-torn place, then you would be empowering and magnifying a lot of negative people with a charge of energy to feed their already enormous and out of control negativity.

Yet to send the energy of peace to a place has the potential to crack even the hardest heart. I am sure your intention would be to send the energy of Light and peace and positivity to all those who are suffering in such a place. Be aware of the language you use during the call and directing of vibration and energy, and always be respectful and take care.

Meditations for planetary focus can be done by an individual, using unakite, in much the same way as above. This would be called a "personal meditation with planetary focus."

Programming unakite

See page 42 for more information on how to program crystals.

For personal use
I ask the Light [or earth energies] to please charge this crystal to veil [full name] with healing for [healing focus]. Thank you.

For professional use
I call upon the Light, please charge this crystal with the highest positivity to veil [full name] with the Light of/for [healing focus]. I thank the Light.

Examples of healing focus:
- A cairn to promote the energy of peace, harmony, and common unity
- Promotes the energy of peace, balance, and harmony in the home
- Positive alignment to overcome the energy of dispute/disharmony
- Promotes the energy of harmony, flow, and common unity at meetings
- Healing meditation and the energy of Light unification

A–Z of important crystals

Important crystals and their energy attributes, with programming suggestions for home and professional use.

Please cleanse crystals before and after use.

   See page 45 for crystal healing program templates to use with the crystals listed below.

Abalone

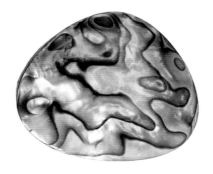

Energetic key qualities: Heals and strengthens bones/the skeletal structure.

Personal use: For the child with, for example, a broken collar bone. Wear or carry or fasten near the center of the break using micropore tape.

Therapy use: For the client experiencing pain/discomfort during healing after sustaining multiple fractures. Use pieces of abalone to place on the center of fracture sites within crystal circuitry.

Healing focus: Heals and strengthens the bones, healing regeneration.

Amber

Energetic key qualities: Opens the heart and settles emotions.

Personal use: For the fearful older person. Wear/carry.

Therapy use: For the client who is an anxious person. Wear/carry or use within crystal circuitry placed on the heart chakra.

Healing focus: Light of peace and serenity, strength and protection, greater surety and self-empowerment.

Amethyst

Energetic key qualities: Stone of transmutation and spiritual connection. Powerful energy field protector and strengthener.

Personal use: Following a painful relationship break-up, program to wear over the solar plexus to release emotional holding and strengthen the solar plexus chakra.

Therapy use: Protect your therapy room/center by placing or planting amethyst at the boundary points of a room/building/land. Program amethyst crystals to create a circuit of energetic protection.

Healing focus: Transmutational release of negative energy; spiritual protection, spiritual strengthening, facilitates greater spiritual connection.

Amethyst chrysanthemum

Energetic key qualities: Opens and strengthens the crown chakra. Enhances spiritual connection.

Personal use: Seek the support of a crystal therapist for crown chakra healing/development. May be placed centrally in the home to assist in the spiritual strengthening of all who pass within its energy.

Therapy use: For the client who wishes greater attunement to their divine plan/guides/Masters in the Light. Use in crystal circuitry with placement 12 inches (30cm) above the crown chakra.

Healing focus: Free-flowing crown chakra; connection to the life plan, higher self, guides, and Masters.

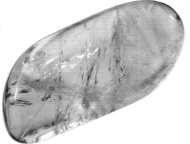

Ametrine

Energetic key qualities: Gentle purifier. Cleanses sinuses.

Personal use: For the child with blocked sinuses. Wear or carry.

Therapy use: For the client experiencing family difficulties manifested as blocked sinuses. Program to carry and periodically draw the crystal across the blocked sinus to move the held negative energy.

Healing focus: Release the negative energy blocks; peace, harmony, flow, and the light of great positivity, freeing from physical pain and discomfort.

Andara crystal (blue obsidian, artificial)

Energetic key quality: Communication crystal— promotes clear connection with others.

Personal use: To encourage positive communication in your home. Place centrally in the home.

Therapy use: For the client who requires clarity of communication for their work/business. Wear or carry. Place centrally in the workplace.

Healing focus: Positive communication, Light clarity in communication skills.

Apache tear

Energetic key qualities: Absolves pain of loss. Heals grief. Releases negativity (base chakra).

Personal use: For the child who has suffered loss. Wear or carry. Place beside or beneath the bed at night.

Therapy use: For the client manifesting grief issues, for example, dark-ringed eyes. Rest one piece beneath each eye during crystal circuitry. May also wear/carry a piece.

Healing focus: Release the pain of loss; transmute and release negative energy fully.

Aqua aura quartz

Energetic key qualities: High, pure energy vibration. Promotes unconditional love in action.

Personal use: For the person who wants to open their heart chakra fully in unconditional love. Wear or carry. Place beside or beneath the bed at night.

Therapy use: For the client who requires to open their heart chakra. Include in crystal circuitry with placement to the heart chakra.

Healing focus: Facilitate the opening of the heart chakra, unconditional love.

Aquamarine

Energetic key qualities: Draws higher etheric light and promotes creativity (throat chakra).

Personal use: For creative work; if you are an artist, writer, or creative, program a piece to place on the desk where you work.

Therapy use: A small piece may be used within a crystal circuit to cleanse/free the throat chakra.

Healing focus: To flow in the highest positivity creatively at this time. Release all negative energy from the throat chakra into positivity, harmony, and flow.

Aventurine quartz

Energetic key quality: Draws one forward in Light and positivity on our individual paths.

Personal use: For the career-indecisive teenager, ask them to hold a piece in their right palm for 5 minutes, or place beside or beneath their bed at night.

Therapy use: A small piece may be used within a crystal circuit to cleanse/ free the sacral chakra. To inspire greater confidence in the timid.

Healing focus: Align to chosen path for life, release negative energy from sacral chakra, stand in full personal empowerment.

Azurite

Energetic key quality: Promotes communication.

Personal use: For the couple/family that argues, place a programmed crystal centrally in the home.

Therapy use: A small piece may be used within a crystal circuit for the client who has buried trauma/ finds it difficult to express trauma. To release negative energy connected to trauma, include one crystal to the throat chakra and one crystal to the solar plexus chakra in a crystal circuit.

Healing focus: Promote the highest energetic positivity of communication for the people that live together in a place; alignment to the four lower bodies.

Bloodstone (heliotrope)

Energetic key qualities: Bringer of Earth energy and grounding (seat of soul/ sacral chakra).

Personal use: For the child who is a dreamer, where that dreaminess is out of balance—for example, cannot focus at school. Place a programmed piece beside or beneath the bed at night.

Therapy use: For the client who is so ungrounded it impacts on their safety. Carry or wear a programmed piece. May be included in crystal circuitry, placed on the sacral chakra.

Healing focus: Ground their Light in positivity and integration through their four lower bodies at this time.

Boji stone

Energetic key qualities: Balances the heart and solar plexus chakras.

Personal use: To balance the person who "flies off the handle" or who "thinks" rather than "feels" their way through life. Carry in a pouch or pocket.

Therapy use: To balance the energy field of a person who bullies people, to promote greater compassion and focus to the heart center. Carry in a pouch or include in crystal circuitry by placing one piece on the heart chakra and one piece on the solar plexus chakra.

Healing focus: Chakra balance, balance of the Light, harmony of the Light, alignment of the Light.

Calcite (yellow)

Energetic key quality: Draws the energy of the sun (joy).

Personal use: Place a piece in the center of the home to promote a joyous family life.

Therapy use: Can be used to raise the vibrational energy of joyousness and positive mental attitude in a person whose mood is generally low, when there is no real reason to be a pessimist. For the "woe is me" attitude. Carry a piece or place beside or beneath the bed during sleep.

Healing focus: Facilitate the highest positivity and energy of joyousness, Light of joy, the Light of harmony, and the Light of energetic balance.

Carnelian

Energetic key qualities: Purification stone for the sacral chakra. Promotes vibrant energy, zest, and love for life.

Personal use: For feeling worn out with life. Wear or carry a crystal.

Therapy use: For the client whose cup of life is "half empty." Wear or carry a piece or place a piece on the sacral chakra within crystal circuitry.

Healing focus: Raise life force in greater positivity for what lies ahead, meet challenges in vibrancy, joy, and enthusiasm.

Celestite

Energetic key quality: Facilitates connection to all streams of angelic consciousness.

Personal use: Program to draw the Light of protection prior to taking a trip then wear/carry to support you on your journey.

Therapy use: For a chronically ill client, program a piece to attract angelic presence; the client should then wear or carry it to support them.

Healing focus: Angelic protection, wisdom, love, healing, support, peace, assistance, etc.

Chalcedony

Energetic key quality: For spiritual connection.

Personal use: For greater connection to your higher self. Wear or carry a crystal.

Therapy use: For the client who is facing challenging choices/path of life. Place a piece 2 inches (5cm) above the crown chakra within crystal circuitry.

Healing focus: Greater connection to the higher self to inspire and strengthen life plan, be of intuition and understanding in physical life, meet the divine plan for life.

Chalcopyrite (gold-colored)

Energetic key qualities: Absorbs stubborn held, stagnant, negative patterns from the energy field.

Personal use: For someone of entrenched negative habit, such as biting their nails. Wear or carry.

Therapy use: For the client who has a stubborn negative habit, for example, smoking. Place one piece on either side of the ears, 9 inches (23cm) away from the body, including this placement within crystal circuitry.

Healing focus: Energetically release from the entrenched negative pattern (such as biting nails/ or other), overcome and transmute this entrenched negative patterning.

Chiastolite "The Cross Stone"

Energetic key qualities: Promotes awareness to the ascension path. Facilitates patience with the minor difficulties in life, keeps awareness to the greater goal.

Personal use: For the irritable and impatient, wear/carry.

Therapy use: For the client who cannot "see the wood for the trees," to more easily find the way of the soul. Program to meditate with/wear/carry.

Healing focus: Help overcome irritation and/or impatience with life challenges, more positively focus on life plan's greater, higher goals and aspirations and to rise above life's difficulties in greater light and with a strength of focus for the soul task.

Chrysocolla

Energetic key qualities: Balances the energy field, calls to divine light.

Personal use: For the chronically ill/dying relative or friend. Place near the person.

Therapy use: For the client who has a chronic/terminal illness. Place near the person.

Healing focus: Greater connection to divine light at this time, more easily filled with and enfolded in the grace of spiritual strengthening to rise above their sufferance to fulfil the soul path.

Citrine

Energetic key qualities: Energetic cleanser and purifier; bringer of joy and vitality.

Personal use: To be more joyous and positively engaged in life, program a piece to wear or carry.

Therapy use: For the client who has lost their enthusiasm for life, include citrine in crystal circuitry, placing it on the solar plexus programmed to uplift and revitalize the client's zest for living.

Healing focus: An all-around cleanser and purifier (personal, home, environment, food, etc.). Joy, vitality, zest for living.

Crystal (orb)

Energetic key qualities: Promotes connection to cosmic energy. A meditative tool.

Personal use: For a sanctuary space in the home to sit in peace and connect to the Light. Situate an orb in a quiet, aligned place in your home.

Therapy use: For the therapist who wishes to enhance group meditations, place centrally in the therapy room and seat participants around the orb in a circle or oval for a 10–20-minute meditation. Use a spoken alignment to bring the group back to being fully awake and aware.

Healing focus: Veil with the Light of peace and tranquility, connect all within this space, collectively connect in positivity to the Light.

Crystal (clear quartz)

Energetic key qualities: Radiates pure Light energy. Light magnifier and energizer. Holds the full spectrum of vibrational Light rays. Promotes Light within and outside the body and home/environment.

Personal use: To Light enhance your home or environment. Place a piece centrally in your living space.

Therapy use: For the client who requires an energetic lift or an energetic detoxification. Wear or carry. Include in crystal circuitry; a placement of tumbled crystal quartz will suffice, 12 inches (30cm) above the crown chakra.

Healing focus: Veil the home with the blessing of light enhancement, purify the four lower bodies, receive the Light charge of positive realignment.

Diamond

Energetic key qualities: Physical manifestation of strength, Light, and perfection. Holds the Light vibration of all the healing rays.

Personal use: To charge your jewelry more effectively to positivize your energy field.

Therapy use: For the client who wishes to use their jewelry to promote their healing.

Healing focus: Raise the vibration of positive energy in all action—thought, word, and deed.

Dioptase

Energetic key quality: Brings fulfilment.

Personal use: For the person who hates their job and wants to effect change in their life. Wear/carry.

Therapy use: For the client who feels downtrodden. Wear/carry and/or place on the heart chakra within crystal circuitry.

Healing focus: Overcome the energy that stands in the way of positive change and greater soul fulfilment, greater positive self-empowerment.

Emerald

Energetic key qualities: Clears the vision. Cellular regenerator. Supreme balancer of the four lower bodies. Heals the heart.

Personal use: For the person "not seeing clearly," who has manifest blocked tear ducts. Wear/carry.

Therapy use: For the client who is depleted after long illness. Place on the heart chakra during crystal circuitry.

Healing focus: Release the negative holding of energy from the eyes, receive the highest positive charge of cellular regeneration.

Fluorite

Energetic key qualities: Overcomes emotional pain, strengthens those with a difficult life path, promotes the flow of karmic release.

Personal use: If you live or work with a challenging person, wear or carry a piece programmed to help you "rise above" that which challenges you.

Therapy use: For the client who has a "block to their life flow." Program a piece to help them release it accordingly.

Healing focus: Positive flow, release, transmutation. Strengthening in the face of life challenges. Empowering spiritual connection.

Garnet

Energetic key quality: Purifies the base chakra.

Personal use: For a grumpy, moody teenager/ student who spends time involved in negative pursuits such as gaming or energetically negative music/television. Wear or carry.

Therapy use: For the client who presents with great anger issues. Include in crystal circuitry with placement on the base chakra.

Healing focus: Absorb the negative energy purification to the base chakra and strengthen the four lower bodies, raise the focus of their energetic vibration to the positive in life.

Herkimer diamond (quartz)

Energetic key qualities: Promotes strength and prosperity.

Personal use: For the person/family working through a period of financial challenge. Place a piece centrally in the home for a family challenge. For personal use, wear or carry.

Therapy use: For the client who has a stagnating business. Place a piece centrally in the business premises, in the hub of the office.

Healing focus: Promote the positive energy of abundant flow.

Hematite

Energetic key qualities: Grounds energy to the Earth. Aligns earth energies. Purifies life force/blood.

Personal use: For the person who feels "spaced out" or ungrounded. Wear or carry.

Therapy use: For the client who has high toxins in their system or impurities of the blood/infections. Include in crystal circuitry on the base chakra.

Healing focus: Ground the energy of the four lower bodies in strength, peace, harmony, and flow.

Howlite

Energetic key qualities: Improves mental energy: attention, retention, and flow of knowledge. Aligns the lower mind to wisdom and discernment.

Personal use: For the child who is a reluctant learner at school. Wear or carry.

Therapy use: For the client who feels a "wooliness" or lack of mental clarity or a challenge to their mental retention. Wear or carry. Can be included in crystal circuitry placed on the third eye chakra.

Healing focus: Facilitate a connection to divine wisdom, clarity, and focus in mental energy.

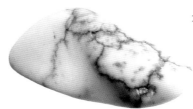

Iceland spar

Energetic key qualities: For veiling Light to the energy field. Gentle continuous light strengthener.

Personal use: For the home where there have been challenges to positive energy, such as illness or the general everyday stress of life. Place a piece centrally in the home, in the kitchen.

Therapy use: For the client who feels perpetually drained of energy, who cannot keep the "cup of life" full. Wear or carry or include in crystal circuitry placed on the solar plexus chakra.

Healing focus: Positive energetic strength and alignment, energy requirements of the life path.

Jade (jadeit)

Energetic key qualities: Promotes abundance and generosity (to use wisely and freely).

Personal use: For the mean-spirited person. Wear or carry or place beside or beneath the bed at night.

Therapy use: For the client who is miserable because they work for a mean-spirited and ungenerous boss. Wear or carry. Use in crystal circuitry placed on the heart chakra.

Healing focus: Greater flow of abundance in generosity of energy.

Jasper (red)

Energetic key qualities: Grounds the energy field. Promotes earth connection. Heals the spleen and strengthens the immune system.

Personal use: For the person who has had an immune challenge, such as glandular fever. Wear or carry, or place beside or beneath the bed.

Therapy use: For the client who has endured a diminished energy after a long illness. Wear or carry. May be included in crystal circuitry on the sacral chakra.

Healing focus: Strengthen immune system, charge with the Light of strength, the Light of healing, the Light of harmony.

Jet

Energetic key qualities: Infinite energy, helping one to flow through the universe while strengthening our place within it.

Personal use: For the young person who does not know what to do with their life. Wear or carry. Place beside or beneath the bed at night.

Therapy use: For the client who is unhappy with their lot in life and wishes to make changes, such as a career change. Include in crystal circuitry with placement 12 inches (30cm) above the crown chakra.

Healing focus: Opening up to divine path, divine role for life in strength and surety, strengthening to soul potential for the life.

Kunzite

Energetic key qualities: Connector of the heart to light. Relationship crystal. Promotes harmony with partner, family, friends, and colleagues.

Personal use: For the child who finds it hard to make friends. Wear or carry. Place beside or beneath the bed at night.

Therapy use: For the client who has relationship difficulties, such as falling out with a partner, friend, or family member.

Healing focus: Positive harmonious flow of energy connection to all around or a particular person.

Kyanite (blue)

Energetic key qualities: Brings illumination, cleansing, alignment, and balance. Physical strengthener.

Personal use: For the alignment of the home/work environment and the people who use these spaces. Place centrally in the home/workplace.

Therapy use: For the client who has to move about in/work in/learn in a challenging or sometimes negative environment, such as an inner city school. Wear or carry.

Healing focus: Positive energy and alignment to a place and the people who move in it.

Kyanite (black)

Energetic key quality: Connects to the infinite possibilities of the soul.

Personal use: For the person seeking their role in life. Place beside or beneath the bed at night.

Therapy use: For the client who is fearful of their pathway going forward. Use in crystal circuitry with placement 12 inches (30cm) above the crown chakra.

Healing focus: Connect with soul potential and ground that in strength and alignment.

Labradorite

Energetic key qualities: Heals the thymus. Strengthens the immune system.

Personal use: For the child/person with a challenged immune system. Wear or carry or place beside or beneath the bed at night.

Therapy use: For the client who is recovering from a challenging illness, to support their strengthening. Include in crystal circuitry with placement on the thymus (between throat chakra and heart chakra). Also wear or carry.

Healing focus: Strengthen immunity, support to greater alignment of the four lower bodies.

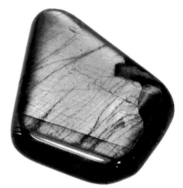

Lapis lazuli

Energetic key qualities: Promotes clear-seeing (the third eye chakra), enhances intuition. Throat healer. Opens a Light channel to the divine self.

Personal use: For the person who wishes to develop/strengthen their inner guidance/ intuition. Wear or carry. Place beside or beneath the bed at night.

Therapy use: For the client who wishes to strengthen and enhance their personal meditative connection to Light. Wear or carry. Include in crystal circuitry with placement to the third eye chakra.

Healing focus: Receipt of soul guidance, integrate light wisdom and ground in alignment.

Luvulite (sugilite)

Energetic key quality: Heals the troubled heart that has suffered.

Personal use: For the brokenhearted. Wear or carry or place beside or beneath the bed at night.

Therapy use: For the client who has suffered heart-break. Wear or carry. Include in crystal circuitry with placement to the heart chakra.

Healing focus: Peace of heart, transmutation of emotional negativity, alignment in strength to move forward in high positivity.

Malachite

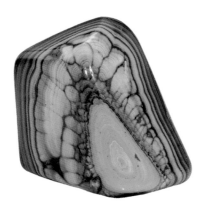

Energetic key qualities: Bringer of Light: heals the heart, calms the mind. Soothes stress and emotional/mental turmoil. Capacity to Light-charge plants and vegetables.

Personal use: To invest your vegetable patch with Light energy to grow vibrationally purer, Light-sustaining food. Place crystal in an empty lidded jam jar and plant in the corner of your vegetable/fruit/plant plot.

Therapy use: For the client who suffers from anxiety/panic attacks. Wear or carry. Include in crystal circuitry with placement to the heart chakra.

Healing focus: Invest land and plants with the high-est positivity of Light, absorb negative energy from earth. Absorb personal negative turmoil; brings calm, strength, and peace of Light.

Moldavite

Energetic key quality: Brings connection to the universe.

Personal use: For the person who has mental focus that gets caught on "the small stuff" or the niggles of life. Use to see the bigger picture. Wear or carry. Place beside or beneath the bed at night.

Therapy use: For the client who wishes to raise their consciousness to have an appreciation of planetary focus—the cosmic picture. Use for meditational focus for 10–20 minutes.

Healing focus: Raise his/her consciousness to a higher vibration of positive focus. Align in Light wisdom and strength.

Moonstone

Energetic key qualities: Settles emotional hurt and promotes moving forward.

Personal use: For the person who carries an emotional wound that continues to color their life. Wear or carry. Place beside or beneath the bed at night.

Therapy use: For the client who cannot move forward due to being "stuck" with an emotional hurt/wound that they find difficult to step over. Wear or carry. Include in crystal circuitry with placement to the solar plexus chakra.

Healing focus: Moving forward in clarity and alignment, being veiled in the highest Light of peace to overcome the hurt from the past.

Obsidian (snowflake)

Energetic key qualities: Releases negativity from the house/workplace. Promotes personal connection to Light.

Personal use: For the person wishing to strengthen their Light connections. Wear or carry. Place beside or beneath the bed at night.

Therapy use: For the client who wishes to purify their home and/or workplace. Place centrally in the area where you wish to purify the energy.

Healing focus: Raise energetic vibration in purity to connect to the Light, absorb all negativity from a place to then imbue it with positivity, harmony, and Light flow.

Opal (fire)

Energetic key quality: Attracts the Light energy of positivity and joy.

Personal use: For the person of low mood, who has lost the zest for life. Wear or carry. Place beside or beneath the bed at night.

Therapy use: For the client who suffers from depression. Wear or carry. Include in crystal circuitry with placement to the third eye chakra.

Healing focus: Be Light-filled to see the joy of life. Raise positive energetic vibration.

Peridot

Energetic key quality: Energizer stone to promote balance and harmony.

Personal use: For the person who seeks to have harmonious flow and balance in each of the body's physical and energetic systems. Wear or carry. Place beside or beneath the bed at night.

Therapy use: For the client with a sluggish digestive system (or other system, such as vascular). Wear or carry. Include in crystal circuitry with placement to the center of where the client perceives the energy block to be or intuit the site of block to the flow.

Healing focus: Align the body's systems into harmony, peace, balance, and flow.

Petrified wood

Energetic key quality: Grounds your energy to the earth.

Personal use: For the person who wishes to connect to nature, to feel a oneness with earth energies. Wear or carry. Place beside or beneath the bed at night. Can be used to meditate with.

Therapy use: For the client who wishes to harmonize their own energy more effectively to the Earth energy, to develop their intuitive capacity to the mineral, plant, or animal kingdom. Wear or carry. Include in crystal circuitry with placement to the sacral chakra. Can be used to meditate with.

Healing focus: Positive Light connection to the beauty of Earth energy.

Pyrite

Energetic key qualities: Absorber of negative electromagnetic energy (appliances, phones, etc.) Assists release of negative mental patterning.

Personal use: For the anxious person, where anxiety has become a patterned response. Program to release the mental patterning that ignites the anxious feelings.

Therapy use: For the client who works in "tech" and suffers eye strain, migraines, etc., from extended screen time. Program a piece to wear/carry and a piece to set out beside the work station.

Healing focus: The release of stubborn negative patterning (personal). Absorber of negative electromagnetic energy (appliances, cell phones, etc.)

Rhodochrosite

Energetic key qualities: Promotes peace and harmony with a focus on solar plexus flow. Heals emotional pain and releases emotional holding.

Personal use: For the person who seeks peace and harmony in their life and being. Wear or carry. Place beside or beneath the bed at night.

Therapy use: For the client who carries deep-held emotional wounds, to encourage release in order to move forward in positive flow. Wear or carry. Include in crystal circuitry with placement to the solar plexus chakra.

Healing focus: Absorb the held negative energy, flow forward in the Light of peace and strength.

Rose quartz

Energetic key qualities: Bringer of peace, healing; skin healer. Veils the energy of peace to those in pain. Key component of the "car set."

Personal use: For the insomniac. Program to veil the user with the Light of peace, then place beside the bed or beneath the pillow.

Therapy use: For the client who endures chronic pain. Program accordingly to wear/carry.

Healing focus: Light of peace; pain relief, healing energy, skin healing, environmental positivity (car set).

Ruby

Energetic key qualities: Brings unconditional love (ruby ray). Purifies the base chakra.

Personal use: For the person who wishes to draw the Light of unconditional love into their lives. Wear or carry.

Therapy use: For the client who has a blocked base chakra. For example, any recovering addict, recovering alcoholic, or recovering sufferer of sexual abuse. Wear or carry. Include in crystal circuitry with placement to the base chakra.

Healing focus: Receipt of unconditional love in Light abundance. Absorb all negative energy from the base chakra to flow forward in harmony, peace, and positivity.

Rutilated quartz

Energetic key qualities: The mending stone for skeletal breaks and bone weakness/disorders. Promotes balance, healing flow, and grounding to the earth.

Personal use: For the person who has weakened skeletal difficulties or is recovering from broken bones. Wear or carry. Place beside or beneath the bed at night.

Therapy use: For the client seeking strength for a life of challenge. Wear or carry. Include in crystal circuitry placement to the sacral chakra.

Healing focus: Strength to the structure of life, strength for the physical bone structure.

Sapphire

Energetic key qualities: Purifies throat energy. Strengthens Light flow from the throat chakra.

Personal use: For the person who has been stopped from speaking their truth in life. Wear or carry. Place beside or beneath the bed at night.

Therapy use: For the client who has challenged their throat chakra, such as the smoker (of whatever substance), or the client who is angry/abusive verbally, or who uses negative language.

Healing focus: Express oneself freely in Light strength, positive energetic flow and Light strengthening for the throat chakra.

Selenite

Energetic key qualities: Heals skin and digestive flow. Cellular regenerator.

Personal use: For the person who has skin difficulties. Wear or carry. Place beside or beneath the bed at night.

Therapy use: For the client who suffers from skin "flares," such as patchy scaly skin, broken or itchy skin, and/or digestive flow challenges. Wear or carry. Include in crystal circuitry with placement of small "bars" of selenite on or near all the sites where skin flares occur and/or the center of where the client feels the block to the digestive flow occurs. (Or intuit the site.)

Healing focus: Absorb negative energy and charge skin/digestive system with regeneration and positive energetic flow.

Smoky quartz

Energetic key qualities: Absorber of negative energy, personal and environmental. Releases control patterns. Key component of the "car set."

Personal use: For important life decisions, meditate with a smoky quartz orb to enhance connection to your divine soul plan for inspiration/confirmation.

Therapy use: For the client with "control" issues, e.g., fear of elevators/will not go in an elevator. Program a piece to wear/carry.

Healing focus: Releases the energy of "assumption" (control patterns). Karmic release. Absorber of negative car emissions. Meditation tool.

Snow quartz

Energetic key qualities: Heals and protects the sacral chakra. Flows peace and Light to the life in gentle continuance.

Personal use: Create a cairn to attract angelic presence to your garden and encourage the beauty of wildlife, which will receive energetic sustenance from the crystal cairn itself.

Therapy use: For the therapist who works with challenging clients/in a busy practice, that the therapist may veil themselves with strengthening Light. Supports their intuitive and Light conduit work. Wear or carry. Place in your therapy room.

Healing focus: Light beacon for angelic presence; encourage and sustain wildlife: birds, bees, butterflies. Nurture strength, intuition, and support of the Light for the therapy Lightworker.

Sodalite

Energetic key qualities: Heals the throat chakra, particularly for misuse of throat energy.

Personal use: For the person who has given up smoking. Wear or carry. Place beside or beneath the bed at night.

Therapy use: For the client who has perpetual, habitual issues with lies (telling lies, living with a liar, or living a lie). Wear or carry. Include in crystal circuitry with placement on the throat chakra.

Healing focus: Absorb negative energy from the throat chakra, realigning to positive flow. Alignment to positivity and strength, enlightenment to integrate the truth in life.

Tiger's eye (blue)

Energetic key quality: Heals negativity to blocks with speaking.

Personal use: For the person who lacks flow in their speaking and usually their confidence as well. Wear or carry. Place beside or beneath the bed at night.

Therapy use: For the client who requires the confidence to stand up for themselves in life. To stand in their own Light in strength. Wear or carry. Include in crystal circuitry with placement to the throat chakra.

Healing focus: Absorb negative energy connected to flow of speech/communication. Charge with strength of positive energy to stand in the empowerment of Light alignment.

Tiger's eye (gold)

Energetic key quality: Heals negativity of not seeing with clarity. Clears energy-clouded vision.

Personal use: For the person who sees life through "veils" (may be rose-colored veils or darkened veils), that they may see life in greater clarity. Wear or carry. Place beside or beneath the bed at night.

Therapy use: For the client who has been "duped" in life (such as emotionally or financially) or the client who manifests eye difficulties. Wear or carry. Include in crystal circuitry with placement to the third eye chakra.

Healing focus: Absorb the negative energy to see the light clarity, positivity, and wisdom of life in alignment.

Topaz (blue)

Energetic key qualities: Clear seeing, clear speaking, clear communication for the beauty of the spiritual self.

Personal use: For the person who wishes to align more closely to their spiritual self and to be the expression of their spiritual self. Wear or carry. Place beside or beneath the bed at night.

Therapy use: For the client lacking self-belief. Wear or carry. Include in crystal circuitry with placement to three chakras—the third eye, throat, and heart chakra—to align to the spiritual self for strengthening empowerment.

Healing focus: To be the greater positive physical embodiment of Light empowerment, strengthened to walk forward aligned to the spiritual self and the divine path.

Topaz (gold)

Energetic key qualities: Promotes clarity of mind and greater mental focus. Clears mental "dross" and assists attunement to higher wisdom.

Personal use: For the person who feels their mental cupboard is full or "clogged up." Wear or carry. Place beside or beneath the bed at night.

Therapy use: For the client with mental "fogginess." Wear or carry. Include in crystal circuitry with placement to the third eye chakra.

Healing focus: Absorb negative energy, align in positivity, greater mental focus, and attunement to higher wisdom. Veil with the Light of clarity, peace, and flow.

Tourmaline (green)

Energetic key quality: Promotes balance to the physical energy.

Personal use: For the person who feels physically out of balance and flow. Wear or carry. Place beside or beneath the bed at night.

Therapy use: For the client who has been physically depleted or the opposite, has been physically obsessive. Wear or carry. Include in crystal circuitry with placement to the heart chakra.

Healing focus: Absorb negative energy, bring energetic balance, flow, and Light alignment to the four lower bodies.

Tourmaline (pink)

Energetic key quality: Promotes balance to the emotional energy.

Personal use: For the person who feels emotionally weak or challenged. Wear or carry. Place beside or beneath the bed at night.

Therapy use: For the client who feels emotionally "highly charged," fits of anger, tearfulness, giddiness, or bouts of sadness. Wear or carry. Include in crystal circuitry placement to the heart chakra.

Healing focus: Absorb negative energy to Light positivize emotionally; balance, strengthen, align, and bring into harmony the four lower bodies.

Tourmaline (watermelon)

Energetic key qualities: Promotes balance to the four lower bodies.

Personal use: For the person who requires alignment of the four lower bodies following a life challenge such as loss, an upset such as theft, or infringement against them personally. Wear or carry. Place beside or beneath the bed at night.

Therapy use: For the client who feels diminished, challenged, or weakened in some way. Wear or carry. Include in crystal circuitry with placement to the heart chakra.

Healing focus: Absorb negative energy; veil the four lower bodies in the Light of peace, positivity, and alignment to walk forward in strength.

Turquoise

Energetic key quality: Promotes connection to higher consciousness as well as greater spiritual awareness.

Personal use: For the person who is bereaved. Wear or carry. Place beside or beneath the bed at night.

Therapy use: For the client who is working through the stages of grief. Include in crystal circuitry with placement to both the third eye and the heart chakra.

Healing focus: Absorb negative energy, veil with connection to higher consciousness and spiritual awareness for comfort in sorrow. Be filled and enfolded with the peace of the Light.

Unakite

Energetic key qualities: Promotes "common unity," unification; the "team" stone. Positively enhances the environment. Promotes the energy of harmony and balance.

Personal use: Bring peace and harmony to your part of the world by placing a programmed unakite on top of a cairn of natural stones, in your garden or an outside space.

Therapy use: Create "common unity" and harmony in your place of work by placing a programmed unakite centrally in a space used by all.

Healing focus: Harmony, balance, well-being. Common unity, unification, overcoming challenge and disharmony.

Glossary of terms

Active crystal A crystal in use.

Alignment "A – line – to Light"—developing constant awareness, connection, and flow in action with and in Light.

Assumption A belief spoken, born of the mind.

Aura The energy field that surrounds any living entity and that which is rooted within their physical vehicle.

"Call" To invoke the Light with focus.

Cellular imprint A place on the body carrying a particular focus of soul patterning, such as a past life war wound.

Cellular memory The pattern of the soul plan (past, present, and potential). Held within each cell of our bodies, may be activated by date, place, personal connection.

Chakra Sanskrit for "spinning wheel"—a vortex of light within and without the energy field.

Circuit A grid of crystals that make up an energy pattern for a particular healing purpose.

Clairaudient "Clear – hearing" with intuition.

Clairsentient "Clear – feeling" with intuition.

Clairvoyant "Clear – seeing" with intuition.

Cleansing To release accumulated held negativity that has been absorbed by a crystal.

Closing To cease a healing session (energy).

Crystal absorption The capacity and quantity of negative energy a crystal can draw from a being or place.

Crystal cairn An environmental structure with a crystal on top to promote positive energy focus.

Crystal circuits Patterns of energy for healing, protection.

Crystal therapist An experienced practitioner using crystals to enhance the lives of others in connection to the soul.

Directing energy "Pointing" energy with intent.

Divine matrix The "perfect" you—the pattern of you according to God's will. The focus we should all strive toward.

Dormant crystal A crystal not in use.

"Egg" A solid mass of crystal, usually egg-shaped; has a special healing capacity.

Energy The life force within and without any living entity.

Energy "attraction" The magnetism of the life force, be it crystals or human beings.

Gem bathing Using the gem elixirs to drop into your bath, that you may enjoy the vibrational healing of the crystal.

Gem elixirs A remedy made from a Light charge emitted from a crystal.

"Hands on" To apply your hands as a conduit of Light for the divine.

Healing To cleanse, transmute, and eradicate negative energy and bring to flow beauty and positivity once more.

Healing energy To apply positive flow of Light to another or yourself.

Holistic reflexology To practice reflexology in acknowledgment of the whole, treating the body and also the human energy field.

Hypnosis A method of controlling the mental energy of another.

Ignited crystal A crystal in use with focus or charged for a particular healing purpose.

Igniting Light charging a crystal for a particular healing purpose.

Intention A direction of your energy.

Intuition "Inner – tuition"—your inner sense and knowing; comes from your connection to your life plan/guides, who prompt you.

Intuitive response To work with the energy of intuition toward healing another in connection with your divine knowledge and guides.

Journey of the soul The progressive learning experience of the soul from life to Light, again and again and again until they have ascended beyond and beyond and beyond.

Karma "As you sow, so shall you reap." The cosmic law of consequence— good or other.

Karmic responsibility A soul promise.

Life plan The predestined opportunities and tests chosen in the Light prior to the life and lived out in the incarnation.

Light Divine energy.

Magnification (energy) To grow and expand energy.

Meditation To release negative energy, to connect to the divine and re-positivize your whole being.

Meridian Part of the structure of the human Light body, which has the function to flow universal life force through the body and energy field.

Molecular resonance (crystal) To show an equal and opposite its perfect vibrational mirror of energy.

Moon cleansing To place crystals in moonlight, allowing the moon's energy to wash them clean.

Orb A solid mass of crystal, usually round in appearance; has a special healing capacity.

Pain Resistant held energy.

Portals Energy gateways.

Positivizing (energy) To make good and of flow.

"Professional" healer/therapist A person who has dedicated themselves at a soul level to healing others.

Programming Investing a focus of energy to a crystal to direct the energy in action. (Asking!)

"Rays" Energy of the divine, blessed to earth.

Sealing energy To protect your Light or the Light of others.

Soul therapist A therapist who acknowledges the soul of the client and works in harmony with this, throughout all healing.

Spirit Divine energy.

Spiritual connection To access the divine.

Sun cleansing To place crystals in sunlight, allowing the sun's energy to wash them clean.

Toolkit (crystals) A healer's collection of crystals.

Transmutation The true release of negative energy from someone or something and its release to earth, directed to flow to positivity once more.

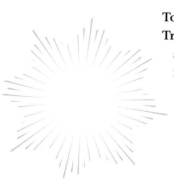

Index of crystals

General index

About the author

Sharon L. McAllister has been a holistic therapist for over twenty-five years, specializing in reflexology, soul recall therapy, and crystal healing. She has taught reflexology and crystal healing at both diploma and advanced level.

She lives and works in Scotland.

Acknowledgments

There are many beings I would like to thank for assisting me with this book. I am deeply indebted to them all, particularly my teachers for the crystal wisdom they have gifted to me. My greatest hope is that this book honors the way that they, themselves, would have wished this knowledge to be passed on. Many people, over time, have helped me arrange this crystal wisdom into *Awakening Your Crystals*; please know that I am truly grateful to each one of you.

I thank my immediate family for their patience, love, support, and practical help; thank you to Cameron McAllister for the additional photography of crystals and illustrations, thank you also to Stuart McAllister for your inspirational assistance.

Awakening Your Crystals would never have been completed without all of you. I thank each one of you from the depths of my heart.

Sharon L. McAllister

Picture Credits

Other books by Earthdancer

Healing Crystals is a comprehensive and up-to-date directory of 555 healing gemstones, presented in a practical and handy pocket guide format. In the revised edition of his bestseller, Michael Gienger, famous for his pioneering work in the field of crystal healing, describes the characteristics and healing powers of each crystal in a clear, concise, and precise style, accompanied by full-color photographs.

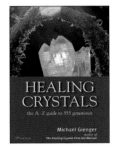

Michael Gienger
Healing Crystals
the A–Z guide to 555 gemstones, 2nd edition
Paperback, full color throughout, 128 pages
ISBN 978-1-84409-647-3

There are so many occasions on which to send our best wishes to those close to us and choosing the correct stone gives those wishes added power and emphasis. This handy little book is fully illustrated with charming photographs and reveals the appropriate stone for each occasion and its message.

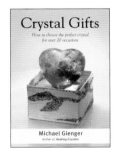

Michael Gienger
Crystal Gifts
How to choose the perfect crystal for over 20 occasions
Paperback, full colour throughout, 96 pages
ISBN 978-1-84409-665-7

This useful little guidebook provides everything you need to know about cleansing crystals—including both the well-known and the less well-known methods. It clearly explains the best method for each purpose, whether for charging or discharging, cleansing on an external or energetic level, or eliminating foreign information.

Michael Gienger
Purifying Crystals
How to clear, charge, and purify your healing crystals
Paperback, full color throughout, 64 pages
ISBN 978-1-84409-147-8

For further information and to request a book catalog contact:

Inner Traditions, One Park Street, Rochester, Vermont 05767

Earthdancer Books is an Inner Traditions imprint.
Phone: +1-800-246-8648, customerservice@innertraditions.com
www.earthdancerbooks.com • www.innertraditions.com

EARTHDANCER

AN INNER TRADITIONS IMPRINT